B. Chirva, S. Golomazov

FOOTBALL
Theory of training
of speed and precision
of actions with the ball
by players

2015

УДК 796 332
Ч 64

Ч 64 **Chirva B., Golomazov S.** Football. Theory of training of speed and precision of actions with the ball by players. – Moscow, 2015. – 143 p.

ISBN 978-5-98724-187-5

This monograph presents theoretical basics of footballers' training of speed and precision of actions with the ball.

Main provisions, principles and methods of training of speed and precision of actions with the ball are enunciated on the basis of researches of individual characteristics of demonstration of precision in movement, impact of various factors on the quality of actions with the ball and transition of fitness in speed and precision of techniques performance.

Materials are designed for coaches working in professional football teams and youth football.

УДК 796 332
Ч 64

ISBN 978-5-98724-187-5

© Chirva B., Golomazov S., «ТВТ Дивизион», 2015

All rights reserved

CONTENTS

Introduction..6

**Chapter 1. Individual characteristics
of display of precision in movement**..........................9
Introduction..9
Components of the «ball feel»..9
    Talent in precise performance
    of any movement..10
    Talent in learning
    of a football technique..10
    Motor sensitivity
    and visual perception..12
The «goal feel»...13
Precision in movement and motor characteristic..............19
Talent and training..21
Resume..25

**Chapter 2. Constructing fast
and precise movements with the ball**..........................27
Introduction..27
Interdependence of time and precision
of movements performance...27
    Pre-programming of a strike motion.......................28
    Performance of a strike motion..............................30
Interaction of a muscle work...34
Cooperation of certain body parts...................................37
Construction of motor programs
of actions with the ball...39
«Difficult» and «easy» movements.................................41
Resume...42
Enclosure..44

Chapter 3. Impact of various factors on the precision of actions with the ball..........47
Introduction..........47
The working load..........47
    Fatigue..........48
    Duration of load..........50
    Frequency of matches..........57
    Intensity of game playing..........57
    Lactate concentration in peripheral blood..........58
    Specificity of load..........61
Psychic impact..........65
    Increasing the responsibility for the action result..........65
    Making decision on action..........67
    Certain objectives..........68
    Use of psychostimulants..........70
Speed of moving, tempo and mode of players' motions..........72
Impacts on motor sensitivity..........74
    Strength exercises..........74
    Using balls of different weight and size..........74
Physical impact..........75
    Physical contact with the opponent..........75
    Use of additional technical and mechanical facilities..........77
    Massage..........77
    Pitch surface..........79
Starting time of training throughout the day..........79
Resume..........80
Enclosure..........83

Chapter 4. Transition of fitness in speed and precision of actions with the ball..........86
Introduction..........86
The concept of fitness transition..........87
Fundamentals of transition of fitness in precision of actions with the ball..........88
Precision transition in training of shots on goal..........90
Precision transition in training of passes..........98

Transition of speed and precision
in training of dribbling..101
Precision transition while using drills
of various functional focus..103
Precision transition while using drills
having a local impact on leg muscles......................................106
Precision transition while using drills making
various demands on displaying of motor sensitivity............108
Precision transition while using drills
making various demands on visual perception.....................111
Impact of anaerobic and glycolytic drills
on speed and precision of players' actions............................114
Resume..117

Chapter 5. Fundamentals, principles and methods of training the speed and precision of actions with the ball............................119
Introduction...119
Components of players' special working efficiency..............119
Perfection of actions with the ball..121
    Terms of observance of principle of specialization............122
    Performing a large amount of techniques
    repeats in specialized conditions as one
    of the most important conditions of training
    of speed and precision of actions with the ball.................124
Development of motor characteristics...................................125
    Reaching the necessary and sufficient levels....................126
    Coherence of work on motor characteristics
    and technique of possession...126
Development of sensitive systems...130
    The main principle of development
    of sensory systems is the setting
    of a task harder than the central one..................................130
    Methods of development of motor sensitivity...................131
Resume..133

Afterword..135
Bibliography..137

INTRODUCTION

Assuming that the winner in football is the one who's more precise than the opponent without losing to him in quickness, or the one who acts faster than the opponent without falling short in precision, the display of precision (quickness and precision in combination) during the techniques performance may be a criterion of the technique of possession efficiency.

In this case it is fairly reputed that the one who performs actions with the ball more precisely with equal quickness of its performance, or the one who acts with the ball quicker without falling short in precision of its performance, possesses the better technique of two players.

Display of precision in actions with the ball is firstly due to the individual characteristics, which depend on the natural aptitude, the condition of sensory system, the presence of necessary level of development of motor characteristics and many other factors.

If it is necessary to perform it precisely, players' actions with the ball are organized identically. Acting tied together, sets of links kick into gear in certain sequence in various situations, allowing an individual to perform actions most diverse in structure, as well as adjust to conditions that may vary over a very wide range.

Motor programs of actions with the ball, formed in certain conditions, may be well realized only in the same conditions. There are failures in realization of these programs occurring in unfamiliar conditions, and the precision of handling the ball decreases as a result.

Therefore the impact of one or another factor may result in increasing of number of technical mistakes, though vice-versa may help towards the increasing of precision of actions with the ball. Everything depends on the extent of players' habitualness to the specific factors impact on the play technique.

This impact is due to the training effect in the presence of internal and external impacts on players, or, in other words, to the transition of fitness in precision of actions with the ball during the transition from one set of conditions to another.

Constructing of training process may be appropriate if there are clear boundaries in which training conditions may differ from competitive ones.

Information on football regularities, specificity of performance of techniques in competitive games, construction of fast and precise movements with the ball, impact of various factors on quality of actions with the ball and transition of fitness in speed and precision of actions with the ball allowed to define principles, methods and methodological techniques of players' perfection of technical skills.

Main principles of training of football technique are the observance of drills specialty and performance of large amount of repeats of actions with the ball by players exactly in specialized conditions.

Since time, during which each player possesses the ball in competitive games, is clearly not enough for the improvement of technical skills, the importance of trainings, where players gain volumes of repeats of various techniques, is much higher in football comparing to other sport games.

For notes

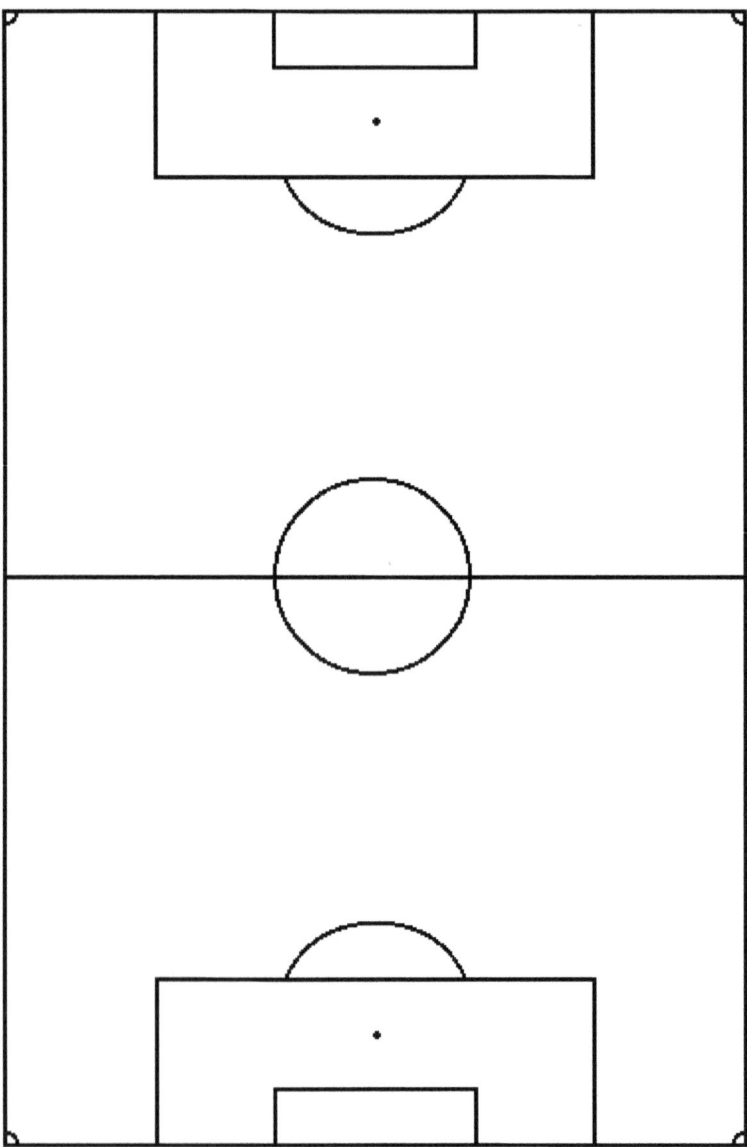

CHAPTER 1. INDIVIDUAL CHARACTERISTICS OF DISPLAY OF PRECISION IN MOVEMENT

Introduction

There are few such star players who are able to do anything with the ball (make assists, precisely shoot on goal, handle with the ball artistically). Nature gifts players with the «ball feel» so generously in rare cases.

There are players who are not distinguished by specific science, but able to do the most important in football – score goals on a regular basis. They are said to be naturally gifted with the «goal feel».

It is necessary for players to possess a complex of abilities and qualities to act with the ball precisely. Just like any other, these abilities and qualities may be inherited and improved through trainings to various extents.

It also appears differently depending on wherever it is obtained from nature or gained as a result of performing exercises.

Components of the «ball feel»

The «ball feel» in football is commonly understood as a smooth, error-free handling with the ball.

Usually the «ball feel» is associated with a high precision of techniques performance and represented as some independent integral quality. In fact it is defined by several independent from each other components:
– specific nature-gifted ability to perform any movement precisely regardless of its shape and kind;
– talent in learning of a football technique;
– level of development of sensory systems.

Talent in precise performance of any movement

Natural aptitude to perform any movement precisely is highly inherited (heritability estimate, measured from zero to one, ranges from 0,6 to 0,8, according to various sources).

This aptitude is generalized, i. e. may be displayed by a person in most diverse movements.

The one who inherited it to a higher degree would be more precise comparing to the less gifted both in shooting with a foot and head and throwing with hands, and would handle the ball better on course of football and basketball movement, in case none of them trained these movements intentionally.

Those players who are more gifted with the ability to perform any movement precisely spend less time to perform techniques in situations when it is necessary to act with the ball both precisely and quickly at the same time.

Talent in learning of a football technique

Young players' talent is often associated with an ability to learn various movements with the ball. It is held that the one who learn football technique quicker is the most talented. It doesn't follow though, that a young player, comprehensive for the new football movements and quickly improving his results at first, would make great advances in the future.

Each person is inherent in his pace of learning, largely descending. The one who learns the football technique slower and sometimes even with some difficulties may be more talented (fig. 1).

Rate of increase in precision of techniques performance by mature players is also influenced by heredity.

Talent in performance of any actions precisely is more important, than talent in learning the football technique, for achieving high technical skills.

Both kinds of talent, which would seem to be closely related, have no relation indeed.

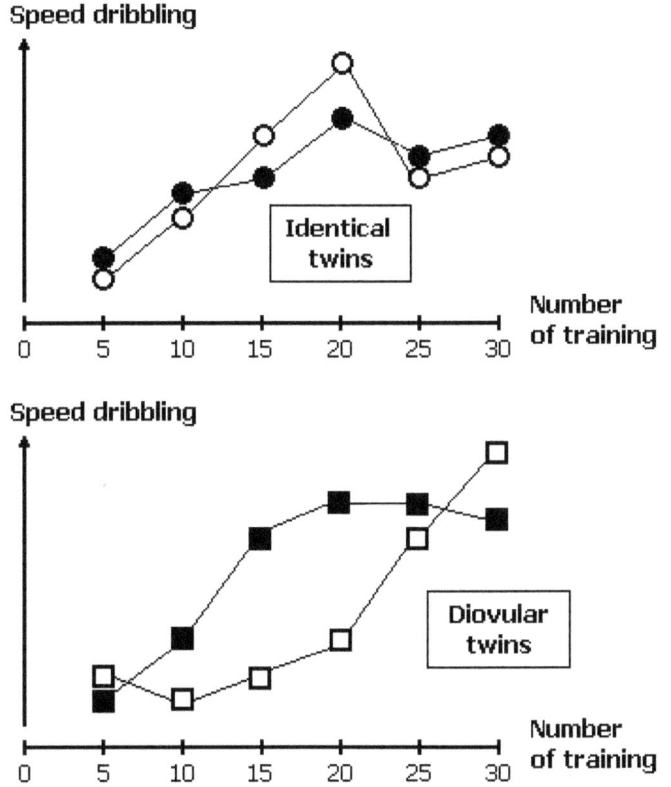

The pace of learning actions with the ball in which it is necessary to display speed and precision coincides for identical twins (who received heredity from one of parents) and doesn't coincide for diovular twins (one of which received heredity from one parent, while the second from another). This points to the fact that the pace of learning is inherited

Fig. 1. Examples of dynamic indicators of success of training tasks performance by identical and diovular twins 12-13 years old while learning fast and precise dribbling

Motor sensitivity and visual perception

Level of development of sensory systems and their condition at the particular point impact on the efficiency of any actions with the ball. It refers both to various kinds of motor sensitivity and visual perception of the ball's position and movement.

There is an opinion that muscle and skin (tactile) sensitivity are the most important ones for players of all the others, but it is not quite so.

Muscles are just performers, providing necessary efforts with their tension. The intensity of muscle tension is set following the sensation of movements in joints, and the sensation of locations of links of a certain joint. At the moment when a player touches the ball the position of body parts may be the same, while combinations of various muscles tensions may vary.

The speed and the movement amplitude of various body parts, defining the precision of actions with the ball, are controlled predominantly by means of joint sensitivity.

There is also no point to overrate the meaning of skin sensitivity. While performing shots with the foot the time of the foot contact with the ball is so short that it makes no difference if the player senses the ball on the foot or not. And if skin sensitivity decreases or increases in sufficiently wide range, it has little influence on the precision of movements.

Visual perception is understood to be not visual acuity, which has no influence on the players' performance of their own movements, but so called oculogyric reactions: pupil motions with different speed and change of the direction.

The precision of handling the ball depends on how precisely a player tracks the ball with the focal vision, because human movements are the most precise in the point of space, where his sight is directed and the head is orientated, providing this point is controlled exactly by the focal vision.

In case the direction of the player's focal vision doesn't coincide with the point, where contact of the striking link with the ball occurs, at the moment of touching the ball, when so called systematic errors in performing own movements occur, which result in mistakes in handling with the ball in their turn.

Therefore the precision in shooting with a foot depends on the head's position and direction of the player's focal vision while shooting.

In case the player's focal vision is directed to the point of the ball where he intends to strike, the foot movement would also be directed to this point of the ball (fig. 2, **A** and **B** variants).

When the player controls the ball position while shooting with the ambient vision, the direction of the foot movement towards the ball moves towards the direction of the focal vision, leading to the imprecise sending of the ball (fig. 2, **C** and **D** variants).

The «goal feel»

Any skilled player can send the ball precisely in the required direction, though not everyone is able to score goals. Those who hit the net consistently are naturally gifted with the «goal feel». To have this sense is to be able to get into the necessary point timely, make the right decision and implement it.

One player may combine both the «goal feel» and the «ball feel», but it may well be that a player, demonstrating the outstanding precision in shooting on goal, handles the ball not so skillfully at the same time, while a player, perfectly handling the ball, doesn't act in the best way while trying to score.

Therefore the ability to handle the ball skillfully doesn't mechanically mean the ability to score at all.

During the game players always have to decide how to play better in one or another episode.

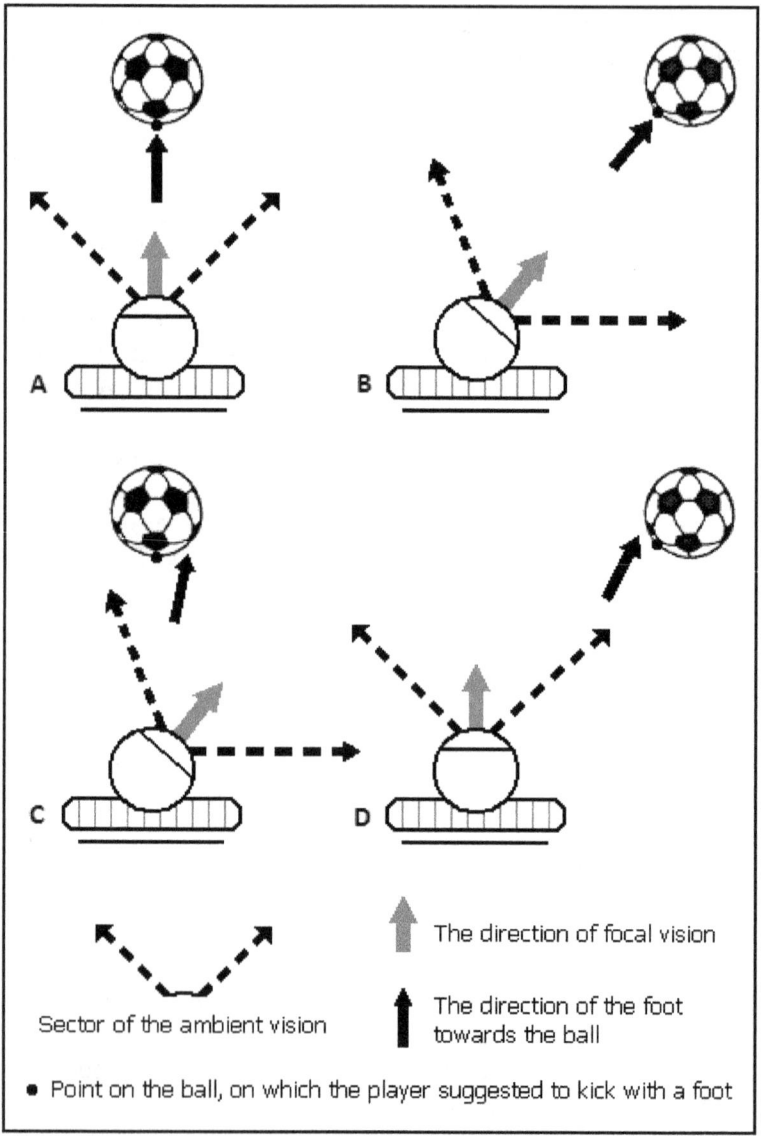

Fig. 2. The dependence of the precision of central (straight) striking the ball on the head position and direction of the player's focal vision while shooting with a foot

When the attack enters its final stage, it is incomparably more difficult to find the right decision. For example, for the player having come over the ball near the opponent's goal it is necessary to make choice quickly: to continue moving with the ball or to shoot on goal; if it is more favorable to continue moving, when in which direction; if it is better to shoot on goal at once, when how to send the ball – with a low or a high shot and how powerfully.

It is important for the player not only to find the right decision at this moment, but also to **precisely assess his capabilities to realize this decision.**

The ability to assess own capabilities precisely (subjective prediction) is the main component of the «goal feel». It is not related with the quality of actions with the ball. Some players may handle the ball better than others, but either may have both positive and negative self-esteem.

The ability to assess own capabilities precisely is conservative and seemingly inherited. Conservatism appears both lifelong and during one or several trainings.

The real efficiency of the player's actions on course of the training may change, but his assessment of possible efficiency of his actions remains approximately at the same level all the time (fig. 3).

Players, who underestimate their capabilities, often hesitate to shoot the finishing shot and try to hand the right to shoot to partners even from the advantage position, while those who overestimate their capabilities shoot on goal for no good reason in many cases.

Players distinguished by a high goalscoring ratio assess own capabilities to score very precisely and can realize the decision made.

Those who has the high precision in self-esteem, but cannot realize a goalscoring chance, become defenders.

Overwhelmingly players are inclined to overestimate their capabilities independently of their age and qualification. Since it is hard to improve the precision of self-esteem by way of training, young and high-class players overestimate their capabilities roughly to the same extent (fig. 4, 5).

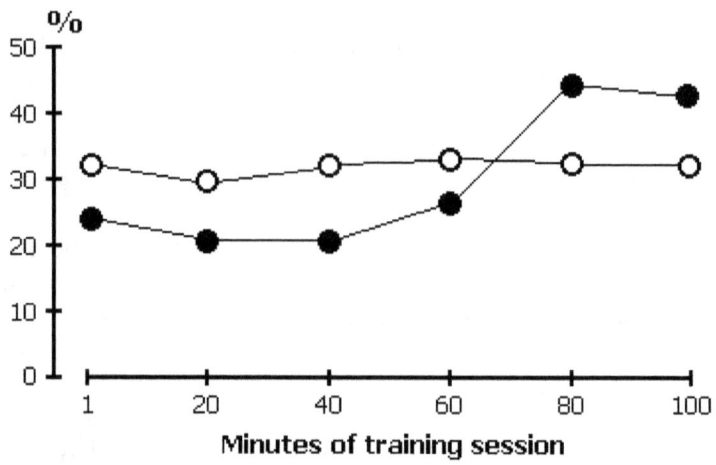

○ Subjective assessment of possibility to score a goal by players

● Objective data on goals scored by players

On course of certain training the efficiency of players' actions with the ball may change, but subjective assessment of possible efficiency of own actions remains approximately at the same level

Fig. 3. Objective data on goals scored and subjective assessment of possibility to score (per cent) while shooting on goal, protected by the goalkeeper, in scheduled conditions at different times of the same training

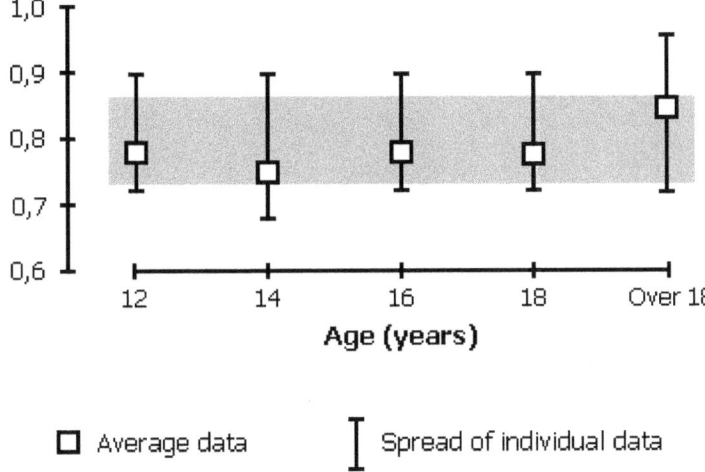

The precision of players' actions with the ball varies with age, though the precision is assessment of own capabilities to perform actions with the ball successfully is approximately the same for young and mature players. This points to the fact that the figure characterizing the precision of assessment of own capabilities to perform motor actions successfully is the conservative indication to a certain extent

Fig. 4. The ration of objective data on goals scored to the subjective assessment of the possibility to score a goal for players of different age while shooting on goal, protected by the goalkeeper, in scheduled conditions (average data and spread of individual figures for various age groups)

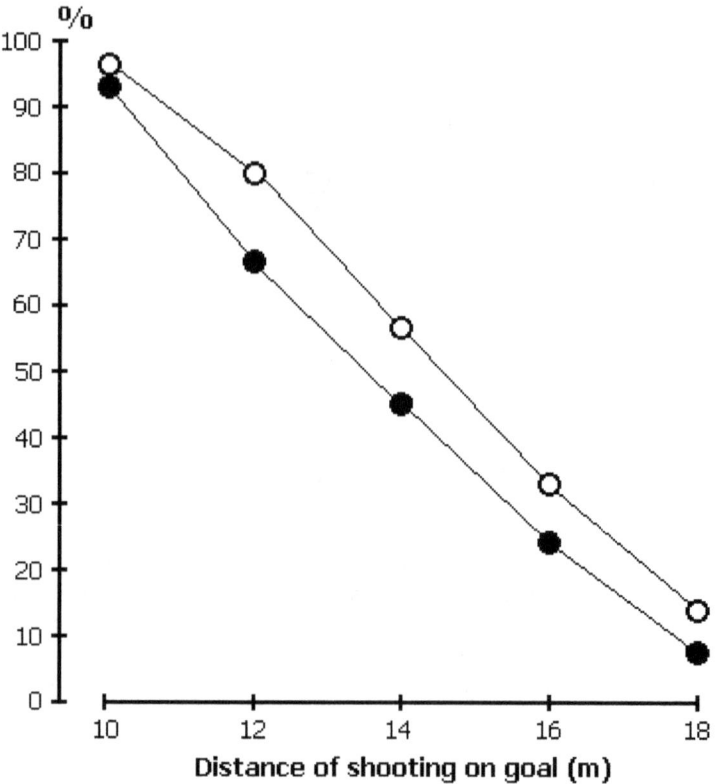

○ Subjective assessment of possibility to score by players
● Objective data on goals scored by players

Players are inclined to overestimate their capabilities to score into the goal protected by the goalkeeper independently of the shooting distance.

Fig. 5. Objective data on goals scored and subjective assessment of possibility to score (per cent) while shooting on goal, protected by the goalkeeper, from various distances after dribbling

Precision in movement and motor characteristics

Motor characteristics cannot hand a victory in football in themselves, and so it is necessary to consider them from the point of view of their connection with the precision of actions with the ball.

Motor characteristics are not related with a talent in performing any movements precisely. It may be inherited by either more and less physically gifted players.

The level of existing motor characteristics has an influence on the precision of players' actions with the ball only when it is necessary to show considerable strength, speed, stamina for performing a certain technique or a bunch of techniques (fig. 6).

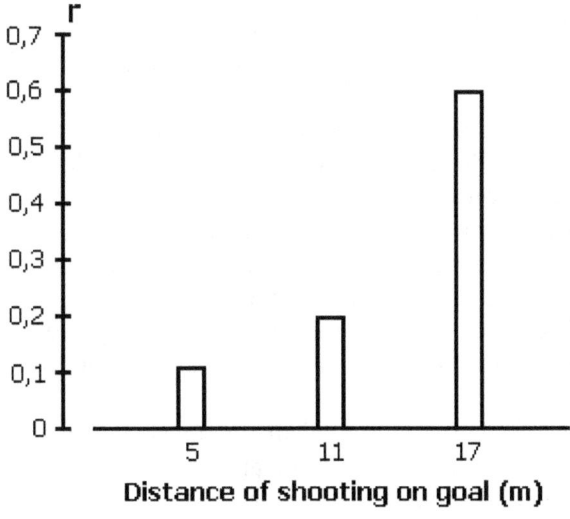

Fig. 6. Correlation (r) between individual figures of players' speed and strength characteristics and the precision of their performance of shooting on goal from various distances

Concepts of strength, speed, stamina, currently accepted in sport, are too much of a general nature.

In fact, these motor characteristics appear in different forms, determined by individual physiological and biomechanical characteristics, and in football display of one or another form of motor characteristics is related with the specificity of techniques performance.

Each of forms of motor characteristics may be inherited to different extents.

Flexibility is inherited in a very high degree (heritability estimate 0,7-0,8).

Of many varieties of display of strength the most important for players are:
– maximum strength;
– explosive strength for performing powerful speed-ups, jumps, shots;
– «slow» strength determining the muscle endurance.

Maximum strength is inherited in a mean degree (heritability estimate 0,5). Generally those, who have more weight, have more maximum power amongst well-trained players.

Explosive and «slow» strength is defined by which fibers prevail in player's muscles – so called «fast» or «slow».

The ration of «fast» and «slow» fibers is inherited in a high degree (heritability estimate 0,7-0,9). Thanks to training a person with prevailing «slow» muscle fibers may become a marathon runner, but would never become a high class sprinter.

«Fast» muscle fibers determine the speed of single movements, which is largely inherited (heritability estimate 0,8-0,9).

The display of this kind of quickness depends on which efforts are necessary for the movement performance: if small, then a player who has inherited the ability to display quickness in single movements would perform any single movement faster.

It is necessary for players to have a trained heart, that allows to deliver a lot of oxygen to working muscles, and endurant leg muscles to display a special working efficiency.

The endurance of leg muscles (local muscle endurance) depends on degree of development of rete of microscopic blood vessels – blood capillary, and on number of mitochondria – «microscopic power stations».

The ability to absorb the largest possible amount of oxygen is determined by the size of cavity of the left ventricle and largely inherited (heritability estimate 0,65-0,8).

It should be stressed that respiratory system is not the main limiting factor of special working efficiency of skilled players.

Talent and training

Nature endows everybody to different extents.

It is easier for more talented player to achieve high skill in handling the ball, as he is initially granted with greater opportunities. However, in cases when talent is not so distinct, much can be achieved through hard work in training.

Naturally-given and gained in exercises makes a different contribution to the general level of players' technical skills (the level of quickness and precision display while performing actions with the ball).

For high-class players (excluding star players) who have approximately equal experience in football this level is determined with inherited ability to perform any movements precisely by 50-70% and with development of sensitivity by 5-10%. The rest of the contribution comes from trainings that help to achieve the certain level of a specific skill technique (fig. 7).

Inherited talent in performance of any movements precisely gives players an advantage. With the same labor inputs the one who is more gifted would be more precise compared to the less gifted while performing learned actions with the ball and techniques in spontaneously occurring situations.

Football is so manifold that it is impossible to work all variants of actions with the ball that may occur in game, and so players able to display better precision in handling the ball without learning techniques intentionally have some kind of a handicap.

B. Chirva, S. Golomazov

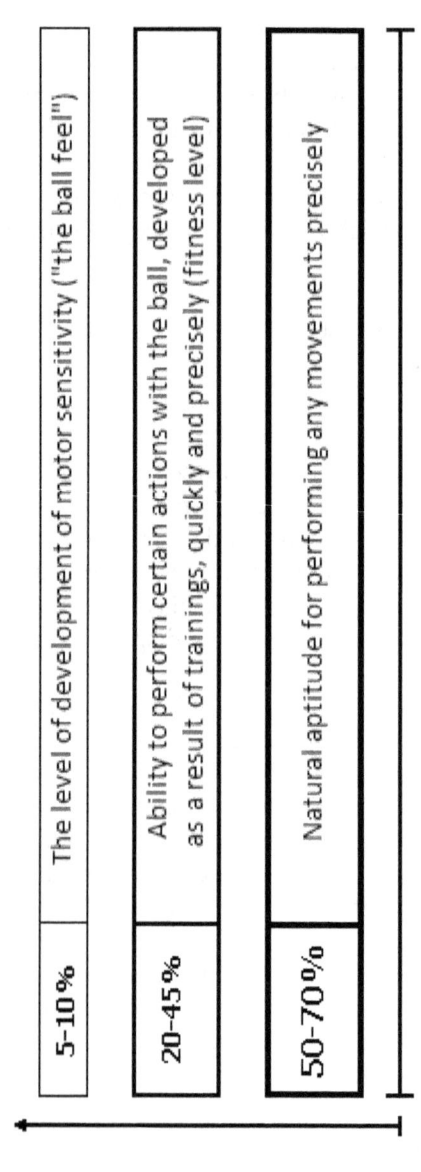

Contribution of various factors to the general level of skilled players' technical prowess (level of speed and precision while performing actions with the ball)

5-10%	The level of development of motor sensitivity ("the ball feel")
20-45%	Ability to perform certain actions with the ball, developed as a result of trainings, quickly and precisely (fitness level)
50-70%	Natural aptitude for performing any movements precisely

Different players may achieve the same precision of actions with the ball to a greater extent by means either nature aptitude to perform any movements precisely or fitness (players A and B while shooting on goal). Players, who have come up to the certain level of precision in actions with the ball thanks to a large amount of training work, may have this level lower than less-trained, but more gifted players (players B and A while performing fast dribbling)

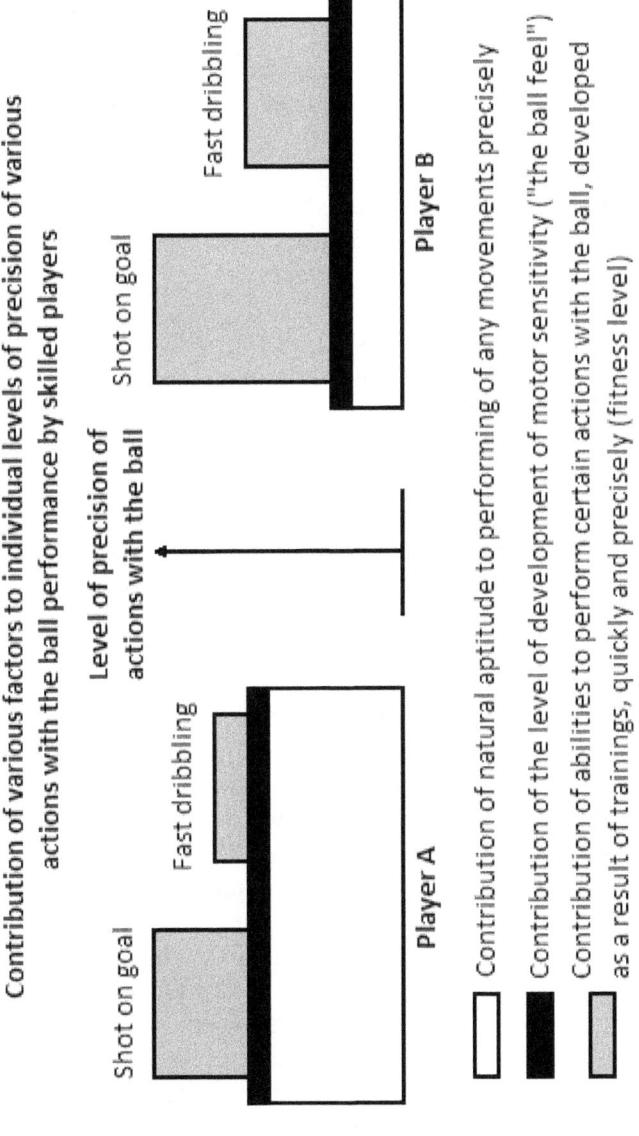

Fig. 7. Contribution of various factors to the general level of skilled players' technical prowess and individual levels of accuracy of performance of certain actions with the ball by them

The efficiency of training depends on labor input, but no matter how much time a player trains some action with the ball, it won't have an impact on the precision of other actions. At the level of high sport mastery training of a certain technique does not result in automatic improvement of precision in performance of techniques, even very similar to the trained one.

The contribution made to the general level of precision of actions with the ball by means of existing motor sensitivity (also inherited and gained in trainings) is insignificant.

The development of sensory systems in training may follow two main directions:
– focused effort on certain kinds of sensitivity;
– increasing the level of general motor preparedness.

General miscellaneous motor preparedness of players largely determines the condition of motor sensitivity. The wider range of movements is possessed by the player, the higher the level of his motor sensitivity, as a rule.

As well as we can't consider motor characteristics generally, it also cannot be trained generally. Various forms of motor characteristics display take training impact to different extents, with approaches to their training also differ.

Flexibility may develop to a great extent, though its overdevelopment resulting in slackness of joints may negatively affect the precision of actions with the ball and also result in needless expenditure of muscle efforts and even in injuries. Flexibility achieved with special exercises may be lost quickly enough, and so it claims constant attention.

It is possible to develop players' maximum strength within considerable limits.

Quickness of single movements increases insignificantly by means of training, while the rate of movement may be developed, mostly before the beginning of puberty though.

Mature skilled players just maintain abilities to display the quickness of single movements and rate of movement at the maximum possible level (individual for everyone) through training.

Players' local muscular endurance may be considerably increased (development of capillary network and increase of number of mitochondria in muscles), yet special, strictly regulated exercises are necessary for this.

Resume

Precision of performance of certain action with the ball is determined by:
– nature aptitude to perform any movement precisely;
– level of development of sensory systems (motor sensitivity and visual perception);
– having rational technique of skill performance.

Talent in precise performance of any movements is inherited in a high degree and generalized, i. e. may be displayed by a person in most diverse movements.

A higher level of development of sensory systems also allows to show better results regardless of what actions with the ball are performed.

Improvements in figures of accuracy of actions with the ball, achieved by means of exercising the structure of movements with the ball on training, may be seen only when skilled players perform techniques which were trained.

Talent in precise performance of any movements is not directly related with other abilities and qualities, including motor ones.

In cases when it is necessary to show certain strength, quickness, stamina to perform single action with the ball or some exercise, insufficient level of these characteristics may become a limiting factor for precise performances of techniques.

For notes

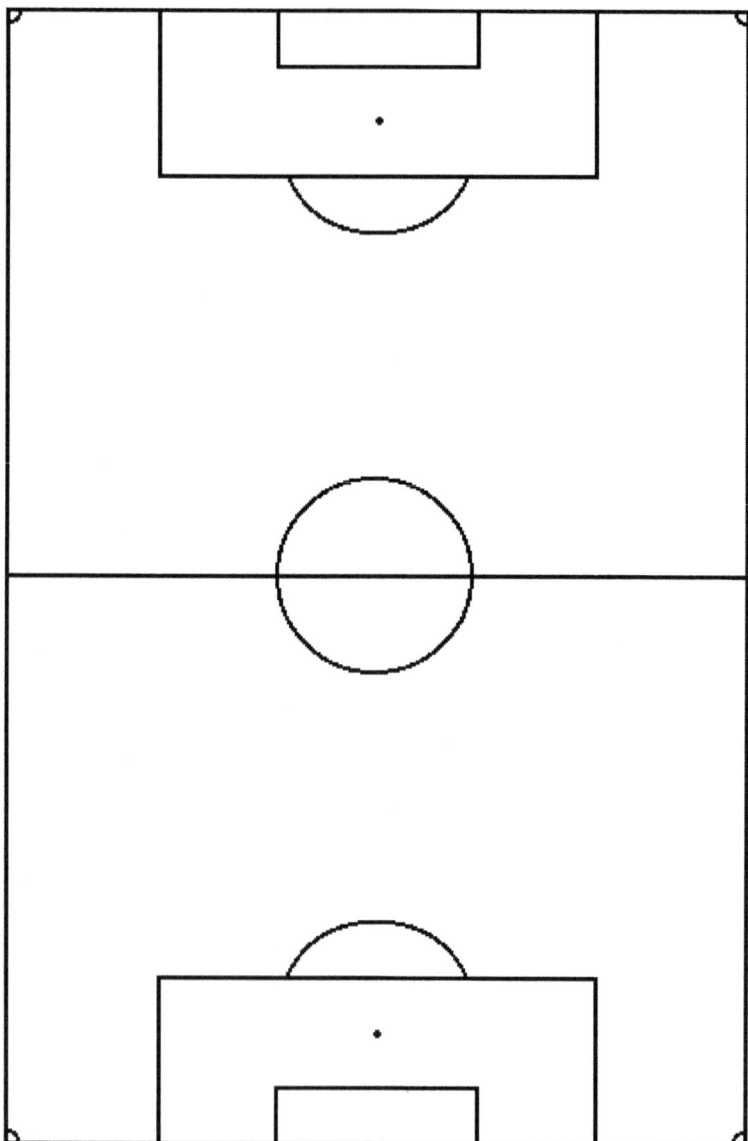

CHAPTER 2. CONSTRUCTING FAST AND PRECISE MOVEMENTS WITH THE BALL

Introduction

Any human movement are organized identically, when he tries to perform it precisely. Deflecting various moving objects comes under such movements.

Overwhelmingly in football players' contact with the ball is nothing more than deflecting static or moving ball with necessary precision.

Quality of actions with the ball is measured on precision and quickness of performance. Usually precision of movements is closely related with a beauty of performance, and perhaps that is why precise actions with the ball in football nearly always suggest subjective sensations of beauty of performed movements.

In some cases, though, actions with the ball performed by players precisely, may not response the established ideas on the «correct» technique of its performance. For example, goals in competitive games are often scored with so called miscues.

Precision of physical actions performance is determined by how the invisible to the eye muscle work is organized, and so movements, that seem to be no different, but differently organized internally, may be both precise and not in different cases.

Interdependence of time and precision of movements performance

Precise reflection of the ball is bot just precise execution of hitting the ball with a foot or leg itself.

Strike motion is always preceded by its pre-programming: the assessment of the ball's speed and mode of motion, defining the time and point of «meeting» between the ball and the striking link.

Certain time is needed to accomplish such pre-programming, which determines where the ball will be directed, and perform the striking motion, which quality determines how the ball will be sent.

Precision of the ball reflection depends on the amount of time player has to pre-programm a strike motion and execute it.

Pre-programming of a strike motion

Pre-programming of a strike motion begins when the ball comes in player's sight as if anew, after a partner or an opponent has changed its trajectory for the last time.

It might be executed as well as possible, hence the movement with the ball may be utterly precise, in case time from the moment when a player begins to assess the position of the ball or parameters of its movement till coming into the contact with it would be no less than 820-840 msec.

Precision of player's performance of a strike motion will decrease more and more with decreasing of this time (fig. 8).

Nearly one second is necessary to assess the position of the ball precisely, and it is too much time for football. So players succeed in assessing the position of the ball correctly by no means always, if they begin to watch after the ball from the moment when it bounce off a leg or a head of a partner or an opponent.

High-class players differ exactly with the ability to anticipate the ball's movement from the way how a partner or an opponent prepare to perform and perform actions with the ball.

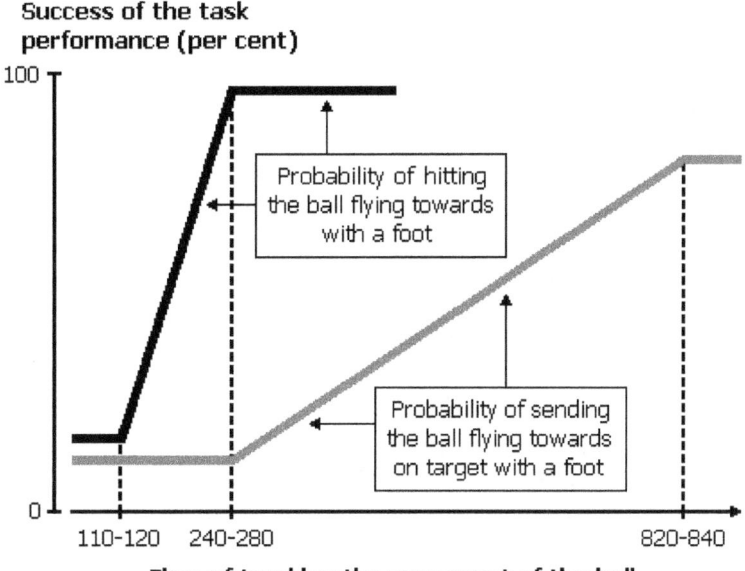

Probability of a player just hits the ball flying towards with a foot and sends it right on target depends on time of tracking the ball until the moment of shooting.

With the shortest time of tracking the ball player may successfully perform movements by the merest accident. Probability of successful task performance (just to hit the ball or to send it on target with a foot) grows with increasing of time of tracking the ball, and when this time reaches a certain duration, player can perform tasks so successfully as his individual capabilities allow.

Time, necessary to track the ball just to hit it and to send it right on target, is different

Fig. 8. Probability of just hitting the ball flying towards with a foot and probability of sending the same ball on target with different time of tracking the ball till the moment of shooting (attempts when a player touched the ball with a foot were considered successful in the first task, and those when a player sent the ball on target were considered successful in the second task)

Performance of a strike motion

Certain time is also needed to perform a strike motion exactly in the way it is preprogrammed.

It is possible to maintain the maximum precision, while moving faster and faster, just up to a certain time limit. There is a borderline set with time necessary to conduct excitation pulse through nerve fibers to muscles and to send new impulses in response to outer or inner stimulations on course of a strike motion for its correction – time of so-called feedback.

Feedback has different levels, and each of them has «own» time, determined by nature, that cannot be decreased by means of training. In case time of the foot movement towards the ball is no less than 220-260 msec, player can still amend the movement by means of visual feedback and display maximum precision he is capable of. In fact, time of leg movement in thigh joint is slightly longer while hitting the ball with a foot.

It is impossible to make necessary adjustments in a strike motion between 200-260 to 110-160 msec in response to outer stimulations by means of visual feedback, while the movement of kicking leg is controlled by means of inner sensations, emerging in joints (by means of kinesthetic feedback, which time is 110-160 msec). Therefore the maximum precision may be shown only is the movement was initially programmed correctly. As a rule, 110-160 msec correspond with the execution time of movements in ankle joint.

There are no adjustments which may be made in movements taking even shorter time (less than 70 msec).

Human movements may be the most precise on one condition: the conclusive part of movement of a link directly providing one or another motion, so called realization phase, should be the same in time.

For example, for performing motion in ankle joint while kicking the ball with a foot this time is approximately 130 msec, while in knee – approximately 180 msec.

In case time of realization phase goes beyond the optimum (decreases or increases), the precision of movements drops (fig. 9).

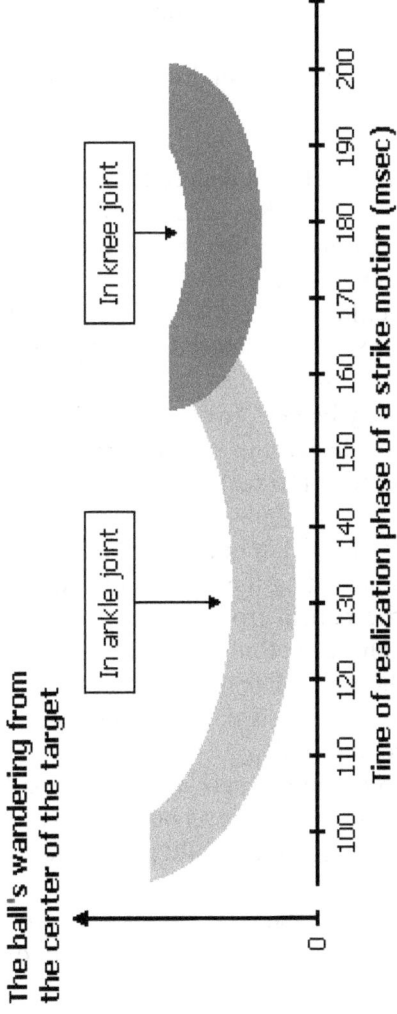

There are commonalities in organization of complicatedly coordinated movements that have to be performed precisely. The highest precision of shots in football, as while performing actions with the ball in many other sports, is achieved with a specific duration of realization phase of a strike motion. As well as reduction, increasing of duration of movements performance in this phase results in increasing of wandering of points of the ball's hitting from the center of the target

Fig. 9. Change in precision of sending the ball on target with a foot (value of wandering of points of the ball's hitting from the center of the target) depending on the duration of realization phase of a strike motion in knee and ankle joints

High-class players are characterized exactly with the fact they always have the same time of realization phase regardless of conditions. With time shortage they don't hurry to kick the ball very quickly, but try to begin their actions a little earlier than the opponent, anticipating the development of play situations.

Change of movements precision depending on time of performance is a sort of one side of time and precision relation. Another is the following.

If it is necessary to display a different degree of precision, performing movements as fast as possible, one would spend different time on movements performance. The greater precision is required, the longer the movement is performed.

For example, a player would need one time just to kick the ball out from the 18-yard box, and much more to pass the ball at the partner's foot (fig. 10).

Precise kicks on the ball may be performed a bit slower of faster by means of increasing or decreasing of duration of the part of a strike motion that precedes the realization phase - so called pre-realization phase.

The lower requirements for precision necessary to display, the less time is spent on actions preceding the realization. And if we invite player just to push the ball in front of him forward, there may be no pre-realization phase at all in this case.

It is possible to reduce the time of pre-programming and time of performance of a strike motion while maintaining the maximum precision just up to certain limits.

Players can improve the precision of actions with the ball infinitely performing them over the same time as before. To this effect it is necessary to pursue maximum stability on time of realization phase of a strike motion.

It would be nonsense, though, if the coach suddenly starts to offer players a challenge to «pursue stability on time of realization phase of a strike motion».

This task is solved by itself if players perform a large amount of repeats of action with the ball in appropriate conditions, trying to act both precisely and quickly at the same time.

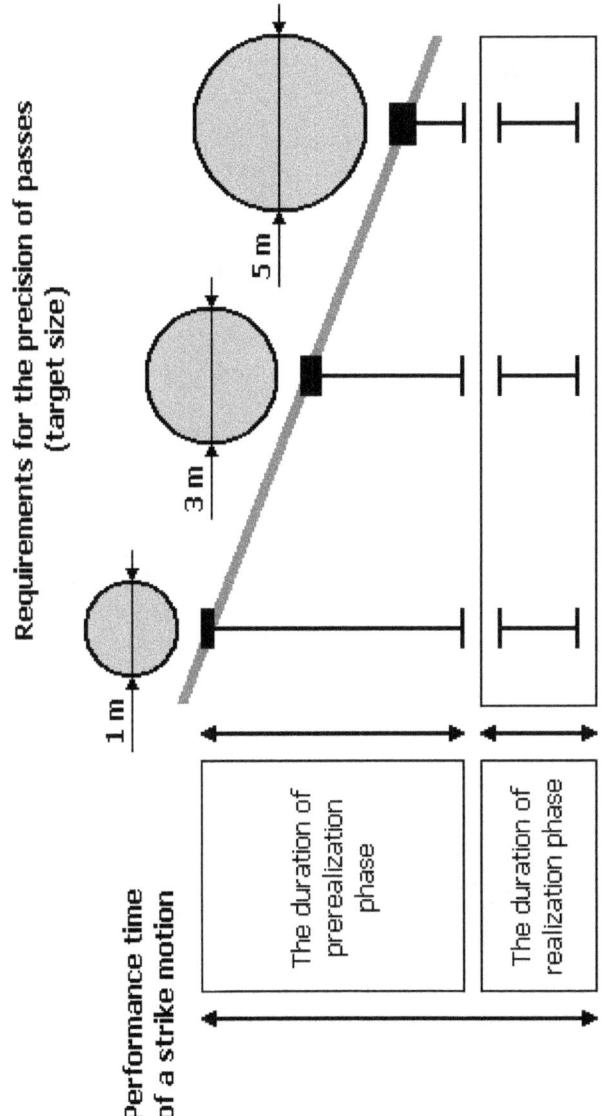

Fig. 10. The duration of realization and pre-realization phases of a strike motion while performing passes with a mounted trajectory with different requirements for precision

Interaction of a muscle work

In humans, there is a vast amount of muscles enabling any movements.

The more complex the movement, the greater the amount of participating muscles and the wider and more diverse interactions in their work.

Physiologists discovered that in case a person performs movements without the ultimate objective, e.g. simulation, only his agonistic muscles, thanks to which body parts move in necessary direction, are working.

When all movements are performed with the ultimate goal, which are generally all players' actions with the ball in sport, antagonistic muscles, working in direction opposite to the direction of movement, are active along with agonistic ones.

Joint activity of agonistic and antagonistic muscles occurs both when movements are performed with a maximum speed and efforts (punching in box, puck rush in hockey, implement throwing) and when there is no power required to perform movements.

For example, a writing person has tense muscles far from a hand, in the area of shoulder and neck, which seem to bear no relation to the movement of a pencil held with fingers.

Agonistic and antagonistic muscles are both involved in a strike motion while kicking the ball, and the higher precision has to be displayed by the player, the greater the tension of antagonistic muscles in work. They are tensed slightly, if a player just knocks the ball into the field, their tension is higher, when the ball is passed to the partner standing still, and if a pass goes to the partner in motion, tension of antagonistic muscles grows even more (fig. 11).

Externally movements of a player passing the ball in various situation may be very similar, even identical, but they are performed with different number of working muscles and degree of activity.

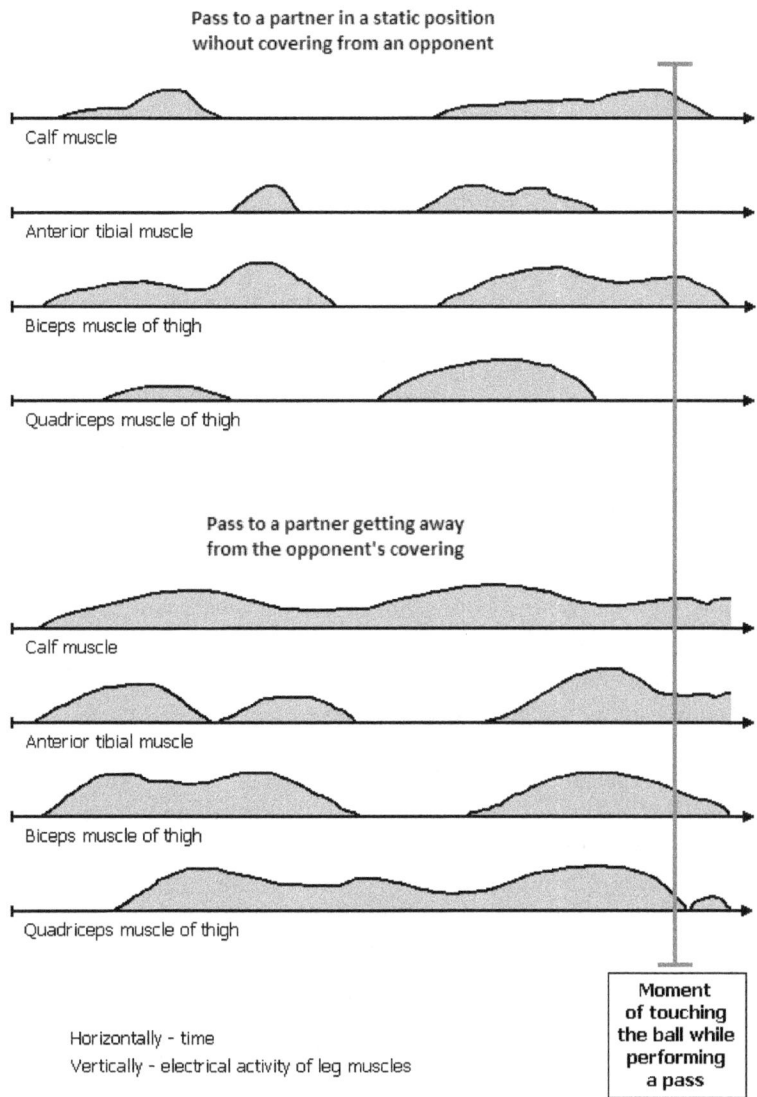

Fig. 11. Electrical activity of leg muscles, defining the degree of their tension, while performing passes with a foot with different requirements for precision

On course of player performing some skill there is, figuratively speaking, specific «muscle talk». Agonistic and antagonistic muscles carry on some kind of a dialogue: «one muscles give corresponding answers to various questions depending on conditions».

Providing the same movements in different conditions, for example while performing a pass to an open player or to a closely marked one, muscles «talk» differently, in local dialects.

Can some muscles interact, if agonistic muscles work and antagonistic muscles rest while performing movements, such as for instance while simulating kicking the ball with a foot or head?

No, no matter how many times such movements are repeated, and so simulation exercise are ineffective from the viewpoint of perfection of precision in actions with the ball by experienced players.

Simulation in training is an extreme case, but in case players would perform any other actions with the ball in training not as in competitive matches, regardless of the fact muscles would have an opportunity to «talk», they wouldn't be able to learn to «speak the language of a real game».

Perfection of precision of actions with the ball is practically the training of coordination of working muscles, corresponding to certain conditions.

If such muscle interaction isn't trained, time is wasted.

In these cases cogitative perceptions of movements, which player is destined to perform (so called motor imagery practice), won't help, as no thoughts can force muscles to interact in the way it is required in competitive matches.

Cooperation of certain body parts

Unlike a robot, a man performs movements more precisely with higher number of body parts participating in movements. This is due to the fact that, firstly, there is correction of mistakes made in work of previous link in work of every next one, and secondly, set of links, constituting a body part (kinematic chain), tries to provide favorable conditions for work of other set of links.

Kicking and supporting legs, hips and body, each taken separately, present some kind of integral whole, in which several links are interconnected rigidly enough.

Motor relations between certain links of a body part, which are commonly called functional synergies in biomechanics, are formed in childhood and retained for life. These are original syllables of the player's individual technical writing.

Here we may draw an analogy with handwriting, developing at a certain point, and however much a person tries to change his handwriting, its elements may always be recognized.

Player may kick the ball so fast it is problematic or just impossible to revise a strike motion, and so each time there are comfortable and in some degree standard conditions for kicking the ball, prepared for the kicking leg by means of movements of supporting leg, hips and body regardless of how a skill is performed (on the spot, on the run, diving, jumping). As well preparative actions of supporting leg, body and especially hips are coordinated with a strike motion, so precise is the shot.

The same happens while kicking the ball with a head. The precision of shots defines not only a strike motion of a head, but also preparative actions of legs, body and hips.

With precise and fast performance of movement with the ball kicking and supporting legs, hips and body kick into gear in certain sequence on time (called timing) in such a way that the conclusive part of a strike motion – the realization phase – lasts within strictly defined time (fig. 12).

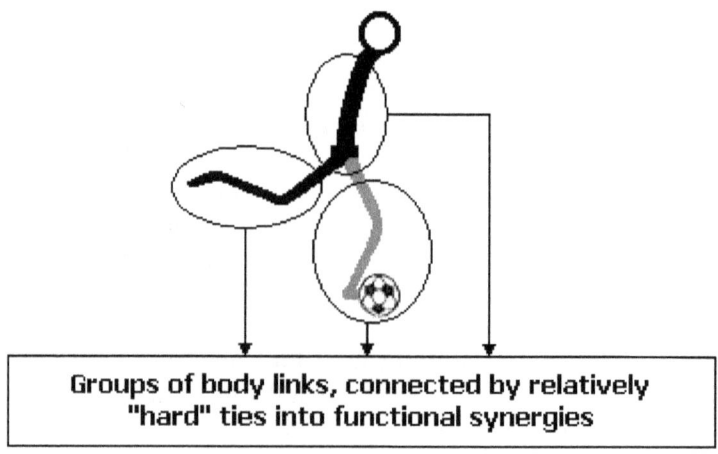

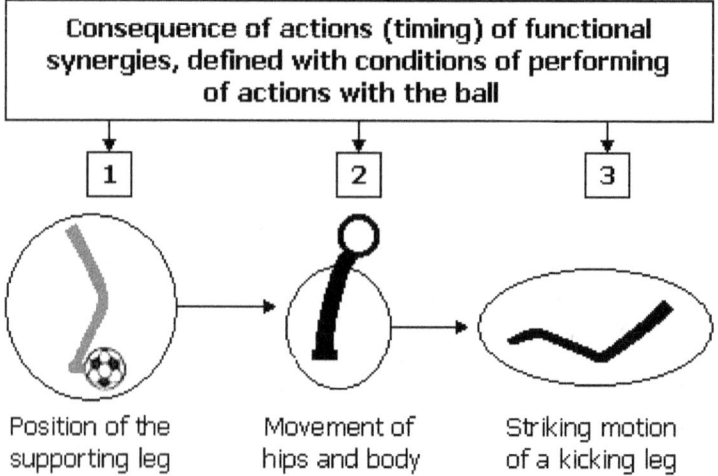

Fig. 12. Schematics of organization of players' strike motions with a leg

This sequence changes in time in case a player tries to show the maximum precision, performing this movement in changed conditions.

However, regardless of the fact that supporting and kicking legs, hips and body kick into gear already in the new sequence, realization phase should still remain the same on time, no matter how fast player moves and with which amplitude he kicks the ball (how far the ball is from the supporting leg position).

The sequence of the legs, hips and body kicking into gear is one of the most important elements of handling the ball technique, allowing players to adjust to various quickly changing conditions.

It obviously better when certain sequences of certain sets of body parts kicking into gear are developed naturally – while playing football. The ball will inoculate the right technique itself.

On course of 11 vs. 11 games, though, players obviously handle the ball insufficiently, and so we cannot do without drills, instrumental for development and perfection of various sequences of legs, hips and body kicking into gear while performing actions with the ball.

Construction of motor programs of actions with the ball

Motor relations between certain body links begin to develop from the very first kick on the ball, which may be performed at an early age.

Motor relations peculiar mostly to more simple actions with the ball, accessible for human being, are evolved up to 11 years nearly, while relations of any complexity – after 11 years until puberty.

Certain sequences of supporting and kicking legs, hips and body kicking into gear, relevant to more complex movements, and also intermuscular coordination develop from 11 to 15-16 years approximately.

Repeating movement with the ball frequently and trying to perform it quickly and precisely every time, players gradually achieve that the duration of realization phase of a strike motion becomes increasingly constant on time, while the time or pre-realization phase decreases. They can display the higher precision than earlier, spending less time on this, as a result.

Thus evolve motor programs of various actions with the ball.

Period from 11 y. o. till puberty is the most favorable time for developing of motor programs of most diverse actions with the ball. It is the time of learning the basics of football technique. All skills acquired in these years would stay for life, and a player would be able to perform any mastered skill until his physical conditions allow to.

Just as handwriting elements remain for life and a person is able to write, until he's able to hold a pencil, so too the football technique remains.

The fact that «technical football writing» isn't lost over time, if a player remains in comfortable conditions in the context of his physical conditions, may be evidenced in former players matches.

While playing with speed available for them, without a solid countering, former players show high skill in handling the ball even in middle age.

If motor programs of some actions with the ball wouldn't be developed till 15-16 y. o., then it would be very difficult, and in some cases just impossible, for mature players to develop them. Hereof there are gaps in technique: one player has no developed shot, the another lacks «the culture of pass».

After puberty, up to 20-22 years nearly, the development of physical qualities continues. It is necessary to adapt motor programs of actions with the ball, developed earlier, to variously increasing motor characteristics and functional capabilities on the individual level at this time.

It makes no sense for players over 17-20 years, already possessing a wide range of skills, to train this skills in themselves.

It is important how «pure» their «technical writing», acquired earlier, would be on course on competitive matches, while this depends on how the technique is adapted to conditions of games with due regard of specificity of actions with the ball performance in various areas of the pitch.

«Difficult» and «easy» movements

Long-term studies, conducted in football and other sports, knock the bottom out of existing conceptions that if a player performs more «difficult» movement precisely, then he would deal with the «easier one» without special training.

The movements complexity isn't the point, it is how well programs of these movements are developed.

In one of experiments skilled players were suggested to perform three tasks on precision. Each task consisted of externally similar, but, as commonly cited, more «difficult» and «easier» movements with the ball:

– shots on goal with great and weak power and with sending the ball with trajectory close to linear;

– passes with sending the ball with a high mounted trajectory and trajectory close to linear;

– dribbling with change in direction of movements with different requirements for precision of handling the ball (passing «goals» of different width).

Results have revealed the following:

– players, who've been performing powerful shots on goal with sending the ball with trajectory close to linear most precisely, might not demonstrate a high degree of precision while performing shots on goal with sending the ball with the same trajectory but with a little power;

– players, who've been performing passes with a high mounted trajectory most precisely, might not display the same degree in precision while performing passes with sending the ball with trajectory close to linear;

– players, who cope with dribbling with high requirements for the precision of handling the ball (while passing a narrow «goal») better than anyone, might not be among the best, when requirements for precision of movements while dribbling were lower (while passing a wide «goal»).

Therefore skilled players have motor programs of some actions with the ball developed slightly better, and of other – slightly worse, though in the context of external shape of player's movements these actions may have much common with each other.

It should be emphasized this provision doesn't apply to especially gifted star players, able to do everything in football and do it very well.

Speaking about the precision of actions with the ball performance, concepts of «difficult» and «ease» movements are inappropriate, as far as the same action may be «easy» for one player and «difficult» for another.

It's easy to perform precisely only accustomed actions with the ball, which motor programs are developed completely.

Resume

All movements of a player trying to perform them precisely are organized identically. Acting tied together, sets of links kick into gear in certain sequences in various situations. This allows players to adjust to conditions varying over a very wide range and to perform actions most diverse in structure.

Actions with the ball are the most precise when the conclusive phase of a strike motion lasts for a strictly defined time. For this body links should kick into gear in such sequence that the last striking link always works in accustomed conditions, including on duration.

Such organization of players' movements is developed during exercise. Programs of actions with the ball, appropriate to certain conditions, are developed depending on what these exercises present.

Construction motor programs of actions with the ball on course of players' long-term training

Preparation stages	General trend of ongoing processes
Learning technical skills (up to 10-11 y. o.)	Construction of motor interactions of certain links, peculiar to simple actions with the ball
Learning the basics of football technique (from 10-11 y. o. till puberty)	Construction of motor interactions of certain links in a variety of sequences and forms of motions while acting with the ball
Play technique perfection with due regard to players' individual characteristics (after puberty till 20-12 y. o.)	Adaptation of motor programs of actions with the ball, developed earlier, to changes in development of players' motor characteristics and functional capabilities
Adaptation of play technique to operating modes in mature football (after 17-18 y. o.)	Training of motor programs of actions with the ball within the principle of specialization

Enclosure

Change in accuracy of elementary single movements depending on time of their performance

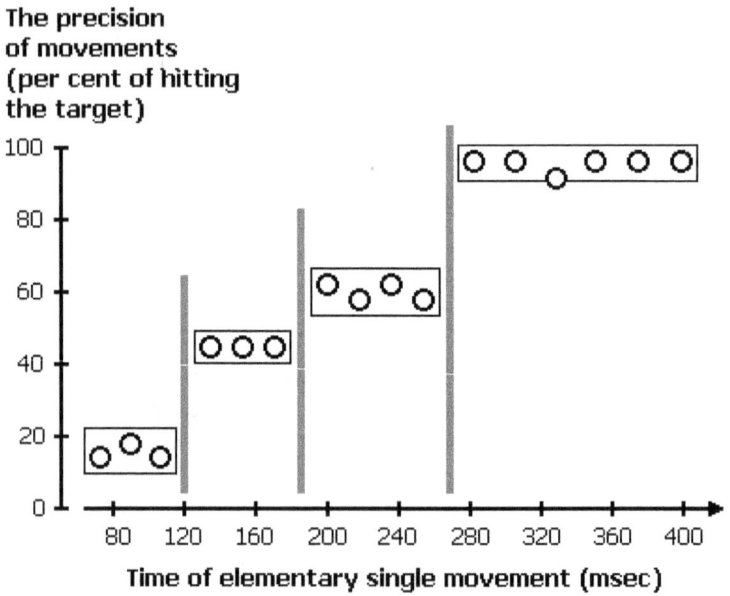

Electrical activity of leg muscles, defining the degree of their tension, while player's performing the same motor actions with different goal

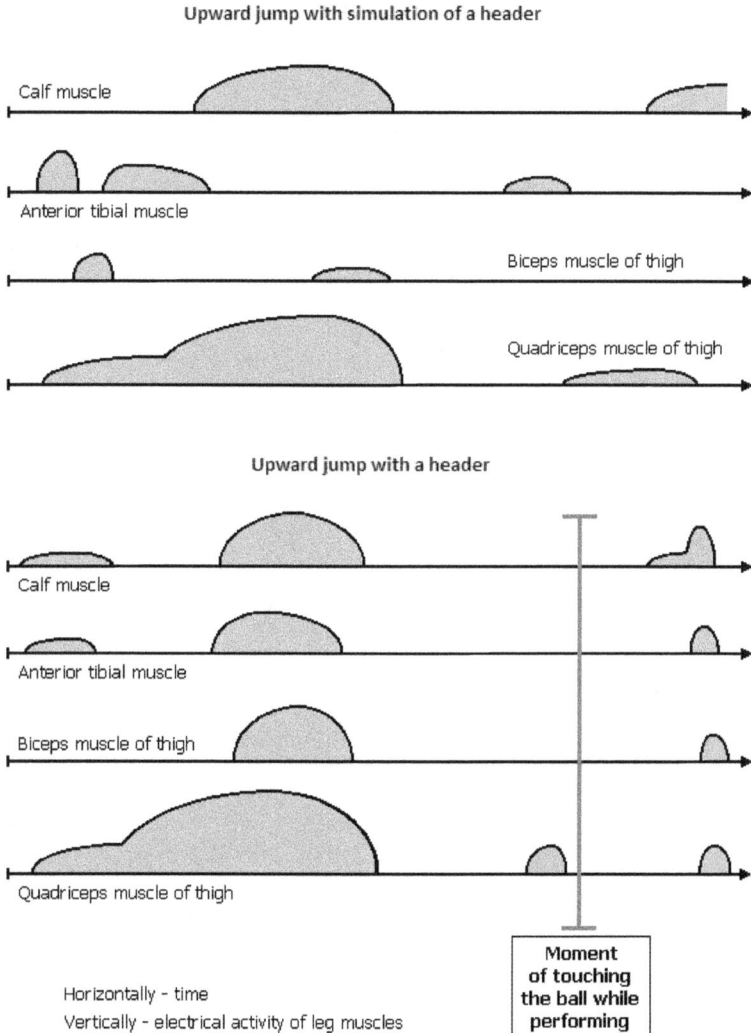

For notes

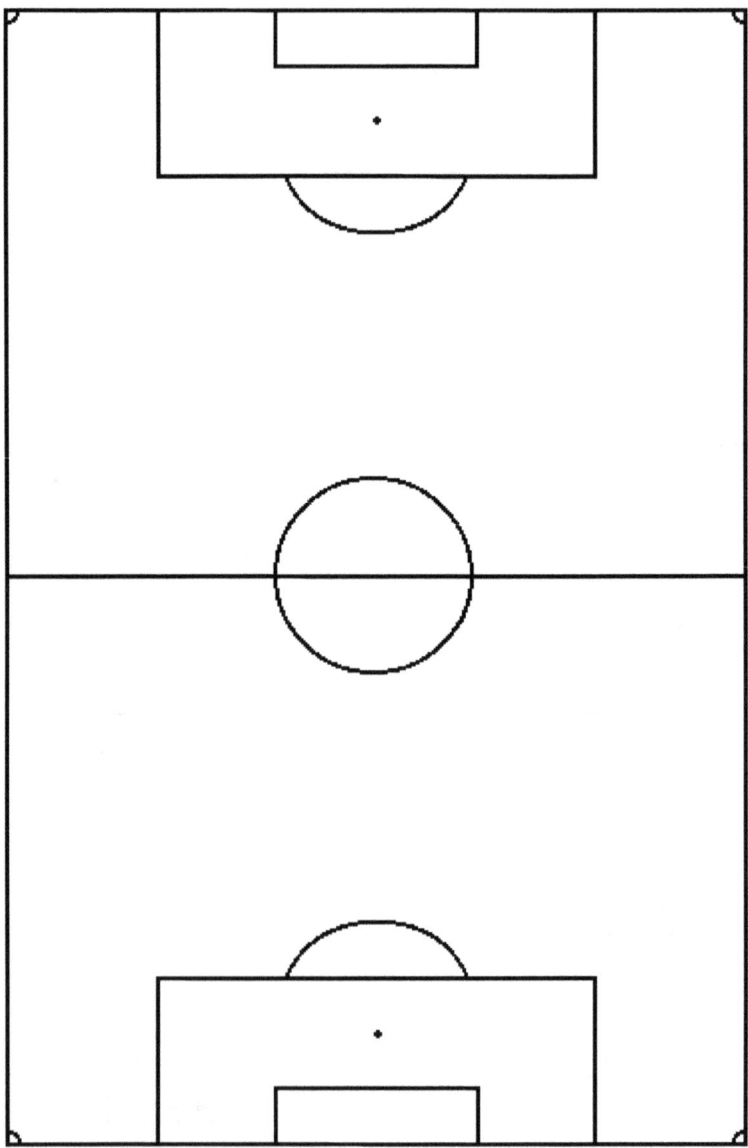

CHAPTER 3. IMPACT OF VARIOUS FACTORS ON THE PRECISION OF ACTIONS WITH THE BALL

Introduction

Motor programs of actions with the ball, developed in certain conditions, may be well realized only in the same conditions. In case player has to perform technique in conditions he never trained it in before, there occur changes in coordination of muscles work, duration of player's movements phases, and the precision of performance of this technique decreases as a result.

All kinds of impacts may result in that player would find himself in unfamiliar conditions on course of trainings or matches. It all depends on whether he met this impacts before, and if so, then how often.

Not only impacts that came around shortly before the beginning or directly during the performance of techniques by players may affect its quality. Strong impact may negatively affect the precision of handling the ball in cases when there is sufficiently long time between this impact and the beginning of actions with the ball: from a couple of hours to several days.

The working load

Any motor actions of players are the working load, causing certain physiological changes in human body.

It is believed that the working load always results in lowering of actions with the ball due to the players' emerging fatigue. The reality is slightly more complicated.

Curiously enough, the precision of techniques performance may improve while getting a certain working load.

Decreasing or increasing of precision of actions with the ball **depends on what kind of load a player got before of after handling the ball.**

Fatigue

Observation over games show that even high-class players make technical mistakes in situations when there is no prevention for them. In case such mistakes occur in the last minutes of the first or second half, then there is a simple explanation: players got tired by this time, while fatigue results in decreasing of precision of actions with the ball.

In very deed the objective data point to the fact that skilled players perform techniques on course of matches with the same precision nearly (see fig. 13).

In other sports skilled sportsmen also don't decrease the precision of movements until the work ends.

For example, skiers, having covered a long distance, often fall after crossing the finish line, having no strength left to move, but even in the last seconds of lengthy work their movements are precise and technique is perfect. Biathletes maintain not only the ideal technique of a step, but also the shooting accuracy all the time. In basketball the maintaining of precision in actions with the ball on course of the match is clearly seen through the example of foul shots, always performed in strictly defined conditions.

If at the end of work (game or distance) «tired» sportsmen act with the same precision as in the beginning or in the middle, does it mean that fatigue doesn't affect the precision of movements? To answer the question if what is commonly understood as fatigue affects or not the precision of movements, it is necessary to preeminently discover what is fatigue.

Curiously enough, there is no clear definition for seemingly natural term as fatigue. Its numerous and sometimes contradictory explanations come down to following in the end: fatigue is the phenomenon of degradation (lowering of precision or quickness) of performed actions.

There is initial contradiction in such definition. If the fatigue itself suggests decrease in precision of motor actions, then we cannot talk about the fatigue impact on the precision of actions, and if sportsmen do not lower the precision of actions, then the fatigue does not occur.

The fact is that there is a gross difference between the definition of fatigue and its subjective representations.

As a rule, players associate fatigue with the sense of discomfort they feel while getting some load, while these senses are determined by the degree of heaviness of this load in the context of physiological changes occurring in the body under its influence by no means always. Results of the following experiment lend evidence for this.

Players of different qualification were suggested to perform two kinds of task:
– familiar football drills which had to induce significant physiological changes;
– less familiar, non-football drills without the ball which had to induce insignificant physiological changes.

After every task players had their heart rate registered and blood analyzed, while players themselves assessed the «severity and fatigue» of the load they'd got on the Borg's scale.

It emerged that players assessed familiar football drills, induced significant physiological changes in the body, as not very high load, while they classified non-football drills, after which physiological changes were much fewer, as a higher load (table 1).

Table 1. Subjective assessment of the «severity and fatigue» of tasks, performed during the experiment, by players

Specific (football) drills, which had induced significant physiological changes in the body	Non-specific (non-football) drills, which had induced insignificant physiological changes in the body
been assessed as a load of a medium «severity» and «fatigue»	been assessed as a «severe» and «draining» load

We can say that players' sense of fatigue during the experiment was induced not with a work more difficult in the context of physiological changes occurred in the body, but with an unfamiliar work, somewhat uncomfortable for players.

Sense of discomfort may also occur while players get specific load, when power sources, allowing to work on a certain power level, are exhausted, while players try to maintain this power level through willpower.

Therefore, when skilled and prepared players make mistakes in actions with the ball in simple situation (in the beginning, middle or end of getting the working load whatever), the reason of such mistakes is not how players feel – either weary or not, but what kind of a working load did they exactly get.

Duration of load

It is generally thought that so-called current fatigue, occurring during the lengthy physical performance, affects negatively the precision of players' actions with the ball, and so the last repeats of techniques are performed with less accuracy than the first ones.

Is everything going that way and during what time players may maintain the precision of actions with the ball, performing these actions many times in a row.

The precision of actions with the ball during the game

To play 90 minutes is the usual load for skilled players in the context of duration of work. Players begin to get accustomed to such duration of competitive matches since youth.

Over the years and with the improvement of players' skills the intensity of game increases, but the duration of competitive matches remains the same.

Within 90 minutes, familiar for players, there are no trends for lowering in precision of their actions by the end of the first or second half. For example, performance indicators for precision of shots on goal with a foot may lend evidence for this (fig. 13).

Football. Theory of training of speed and precision of actions with the ball by players

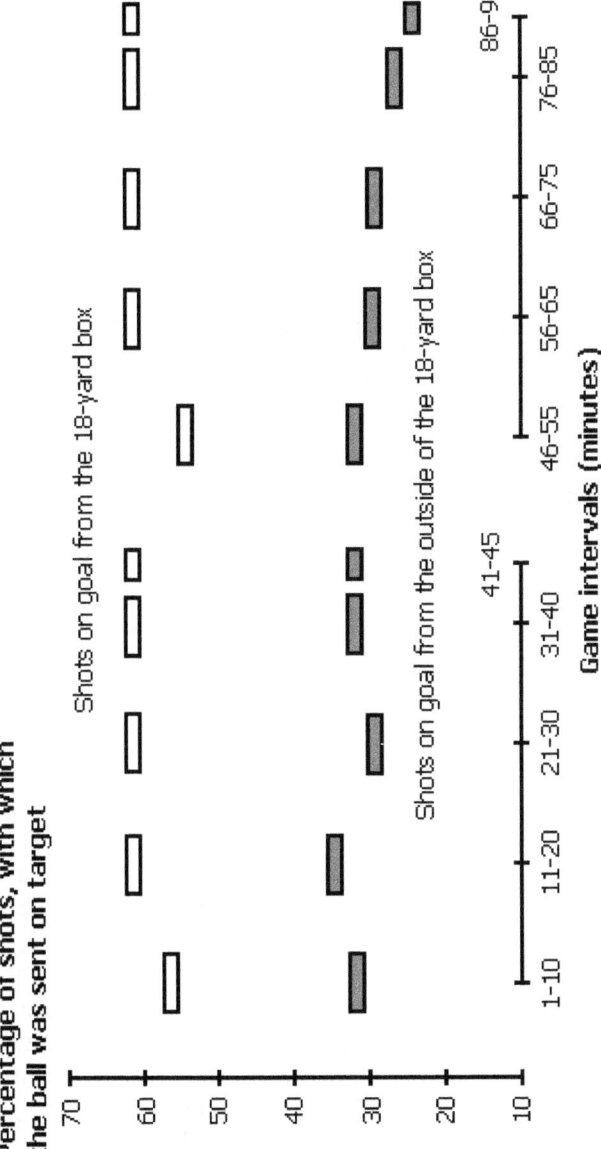

Fig. 13. The dynamics of precision of players performing shots on goal with a foot from different areas of the pitch (percentage of shots on target) in different periods of the game in World Cup matches

In the beginning of the half there is some increase in the precision of shots, while further, during the first and second half, the percentage of hitting the target stays almost unchanged.

Generally the percentage of balls hitting the target after kicks with a foot grows, albeit insignificantly, from the 1st to 90th minute.

It also should be noticed that the percentage of balls hitting the target after shots from the outside of the 18-yard box slightly lowers by the end of the game. This can be explained by the fact that players of teams seeking the preservation of score often shoot on goal from the distance in the last minutes, not so much concerning about the precision, as having the gaining time in mind.

In certain competitions the provision is made for additional 30 minutes. At this moment there may be some increase of number of technical mistakes, as players have to play the additional time rarely enough, and such a load is somewhat unfamiliar.

The precision of actions with the ball during the exercise

While acting with low power, players may perform techniques for a very long time while maintaining the precision of performance. It is confirmed by results of the following experiment.

Players were suggested to shoot on target with a foot and with a static ball, repeating the task until they would refuse to perform them because of lack of strength.

Each player performed up to 600-700 shots in 1-1,5 hours, with the last shots didn't differ from the first ones on precision.

Moreover, when players found themselves in defatigation and therefore refused to perform the task, yet shot several times more, these conclusive shot didn't differ on precision from those performed in the middle of the task.

When players were suggested to perform the same shots, with an additional load though (with short and the most powerful speed-ups between repeats), they refuse the task after 80-100 shots already. Though while performing this task, after first 10-15 attempts players maintained the precision of shots at the same level till the refusal of the task performance, with the level of precision was higher that while shooting without a load (fig. 14).

It also was registered that biomechanical figures of shot technique during this experiment remain the same for the duration of shots performance both with an additional load and without it (see the annex to chapter).

The precision of players' actions with the ball remains at the same level regardless of the duration of exercise, though this duration is limited with the capacity of work performed.

The precision of actions with the ball while getting the load of a maximum and almost maximum capacity once

Players may act with an ultimate output no longer than 6-8 seconds, as far as exactly in this time leg muscles use the «fast fuel» – adenosine triphosphoric acid (ATA) and creatine phosphate (Pcr).

If players try to continue to act with an ultimate output further, muscles work quite differently while touching the ball: intermuscular coordination and sequence of certain body parts engagement into strike motion change, quickness and precision of skills performance decrease as a result.

That's why players from top teams over the world slow down and wait for partners' help after performing a powerful breakthrough with the ball for 40-50 meters while seemingly having an opportunity to move forward.

It may be not accident that runners in 110-meter hurdles have so-called «sore hurdle» – eighth in succession. Even high class hurdlers often knock it down, seemingly because of lowering in the precision of actions, which occurs after 8 seconds of running approximately.

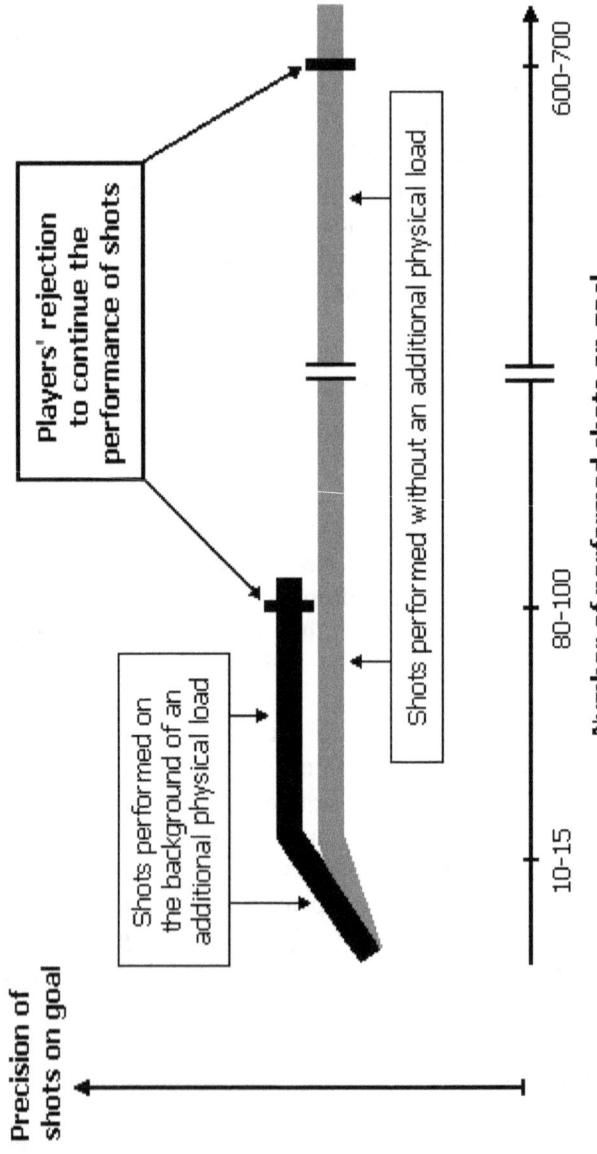

Fig. 14. The dynamics of precision of players performing shots on goal with a foot for a long period of time

The duration of work with a maximum capacity is determined by nature (some have it more, some have it less), and it cannot be increased by training. Therefore in competitions of sprinters of equal class not everyone who wins in 100 meters, wins 60 meters, and not everyone who wins in 60 and 100 meters, outruns opponents at 200 meters.

When players from the youth team who'd been training together for five years were suggested to run with a maximum speed without the ball at different distances (from 30 to 70 meters in various attempts) before performing passes with a mounted trajectory and dribbling with change of direction, the following emerged.

Every player has his «own» distance, after running of which with an ultimate output he is able then to act with the ball well (quickly and precisely).

Players who were able to handle the ball flawlessly after running with an ultimate output at 70 meters, acted with the ball with the same precision after performing the most powerful speed-ups without the ball at shorter distances (fig. 15).

Generally the duration of episodes that players spend in games with an output close to maximum doesn't exceed 20 seconds. In training player are often suggested to work in such mode for a longer time.

After 30-35 seconds of work with an output close to maximum players start to act at significantly lower speed.

In this time the exhaustion of anaerobic energy sources, through which the work of an output close to the maximum was performed, occurs, and players have to spend much longer time on performing every technique to maintain the precision.

Until such energy source exhaustion happens (within 30-35 seconds), players maintain the precision of actions with the ball at the same level though.

Note that for 400 meters runners the last 50 meters are the most difficult. Glycogen reserves in muscles are exhausted at this time, and sportsmen are forced to make enormous efforts to maintain the precision and quickness of running movements.

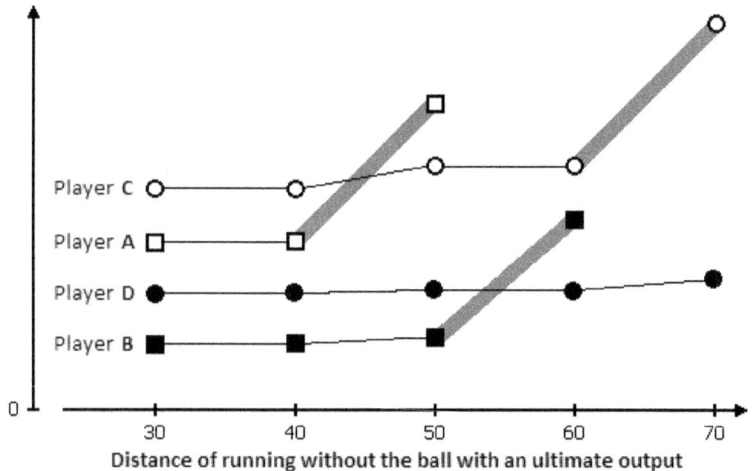

For the player A there is considerable increase of time of performance of actions with the ball, demanding the display of speed and precision of actions, after running without the ball with an ultimate output at 50 meters and more

For the player B there is considerable increase of time of performance of actions with the ball, demanding the display of speed and precision of actions, after running without the ball with an ultimate output at 60 meters and more

For the player C there is considerable increase of time of performance of actions with the ball, demanding the display of speed and precision of actions, after running without the ball with an ultimate output at 70 meters and more

For the player D there is no considerable increase of time of performance of actions with the ball, demanding the display of speed and precision of actions, after running without the ball with an ultimate output at 70 meters and more

Fig. 15. Examples of players differ in individual capabilities to maintain the speed and precision of actions with the ball after performing a work different in duration with an ultimate output (running without the ball with an ultimate output at different distance)

Frequency of matches

In many cases the reduction in the quality of actions with the ball are explained with that players had to play in competitive matches frequently, they are tired and so began to make more mistakes.

But the frequency of matches itself is not the main reason for increasing of number of technical mistakes. At present the world's best players participate in 50-60 competitive matches over the season, appearing two times a week for sufficiently long periods of time. The reality is that such frequency of matches is quite acceptable, and moreover, it contributes to players' functional capabilities and technical prowess growth at most.

The main reason for reduction in the quality of play in cases then players perform frequently is not that they have to play frequently, but that they have to perform unusually often for them.

If players get used to play only once a week, then two matches a week on course of several weeks are obviously excessive load for them, it is clearly unfamiliar and would result in reduction in the quality of actions with the ball.

Intensity of game playing

One of the factors that may force players to make more mistakes while performing techniques is the increased intensity of actions and the density of contests. This is due to the fact that players have to perform far from the fitness shape they are used to, if such game mode is really unusual for them.

However, a team supposing to play with increased intensity should be ready to it first and foremost, otherwise such play manner may come as a surprise for players of this team.

Not only more difficult, but also easier conditions may turn out to be somewhat unfamiliar for certain players, when they have to act with intensity much lower than the one they are used to, and they don't get their regular load.

There are known cases when players who act as a team powerhouse were suggested to play as a center-half covering partners for the team's benefit. In this situation there was no need to run as much as they're used to, while they received the ball by far less frequently than usually. Generally these players, feeling themselves fresh like never before, entirely coped with their task in these cases, though felt slightly out of place.

Slow game with a large number of pauses and breaks is uncomfortable for the team used to play fast. In these cases the decreasing of precision of players' actions with the ball, though imperceptible to the eye, still occurs.

Therefore, when players find themselves in easier conditions compared to those they usually train and play in, they should generally feel themselves less confident while handling the ball, if these easy conditions are obviously unfamiliar for them.

It doesn't mean though, that competitive games should be played in a way that establishes facilitated conditions for the opponent, because players for whom such conditions would be familiar are unlikely to be found. Contrarily, a sharp decrease in precision of actions with the ball should be expected when players get into more difficult conditions comparing to those they are used to train and play in, as more difficult conditions are exactly unfamiliar for them most probably. And if it is possible to establish such condition for opponents, they would make much more mistakes.

Lactate concentration in peripheral blood

One of indicators of physiological changes occurring in sportsman's body while getting the working load is change of lactate concentration in peripheral blood.

According to so-called acidulation theory it is thought that increase of lactate level in blood results in decrease in the precision of movements. Special experiments were conducted to find out wherever this is the case.

Interrelation between the lactate concentration in peripheral blood and the precision of players' action with the ball was considered from two points:

– how the dynamics of lactate concentration and the dynamics of the precision of actions with the ball while players getting a single load are related;

– how does the increased lactate concentration impact on the precision of actions with the ball of players of different qualification.

In the first experiment the following task was suggested to high class players: to perform actions with the ball with high intensity, resulting in sufficient increasing of lactate in peripheral blood.

Before and after the task (during a warm-up and pause of active rest) players were performing the sane actions with the ball, although with a low intensity.

During the task performance and also during a warm-up and rest pause the indicators of lactate concentrations were registered.

It emerged that there were no interrelation between the dynamics of indicators, defining the quality of actions with the ball (the precision of shots on goal, display of speed and precision while dribbling and passes), and the dynamics of the lactate concentration: after the lactate concentrations had reached high values, players continued to perform the task without lowering the quality of actions with the ball (fig. 16).

In the second experiment players of different qualification were suggested to perform the same football drills that should result in increased lactate concentration.

Briefly after the beginning of these drills performance less qualified players began to make more and more mistakes, while more qualified players acted with the ball with relatively the same precision until the end of task.

Change in quickness and precision of actions with the ball is firstly defined with a degree of players' habitualness to work in conditions of a certain level of the lactate concentration in peripheral blood.

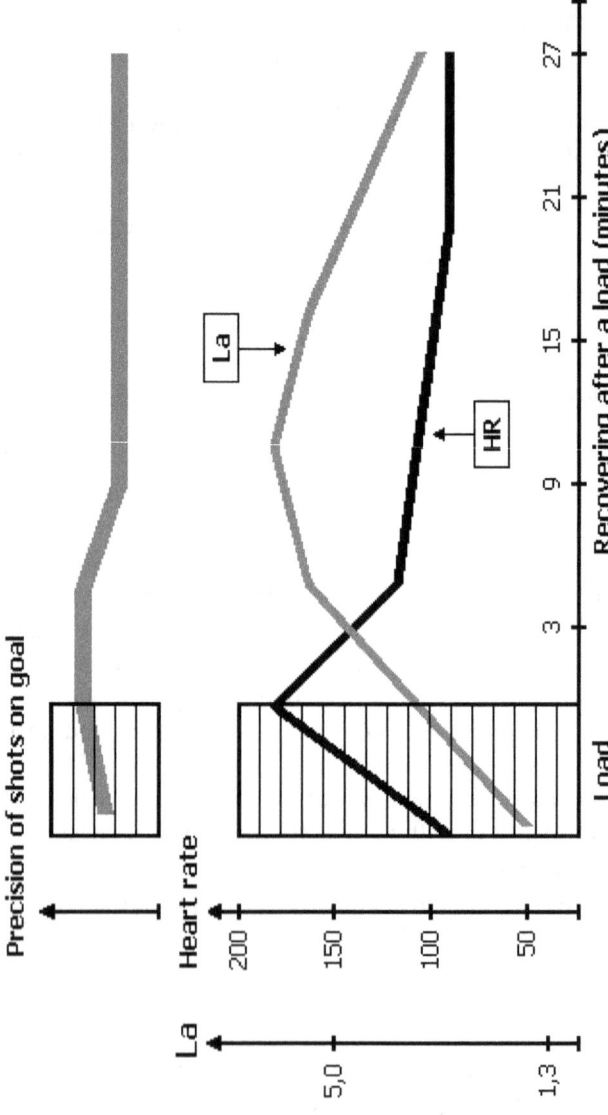

Fig. 16. The dynamics of the lactate concentration (La) in peripheral blood, heart rate and the precision of shots on goal with a foot on course of skilled players getting the specific load (football drills) and during the recovery period

Specificity of load

Physiological changes of different magnitude, occurring in the body after getting working load, in some cases may result in lowering of quality of actions with the ball, while in other – help towards its increasing.

Researches with players of different qualification have revealed that the precision of actions with the ball firstly depends on how physiological changes, occurred in the body, are familiar or unfamiliar for them, how familiar or unfamiliar the load, which induced these changes, is.

In one of experiments players were suggested to perform two tasks (same on intensity, duration, work and rest intervals) which should induce quite the same physiological changes. One task consisted of drills with the ball familiar for players, another – of drills without the ball unfamiliar for them (nonspecific). Before and after performing tasks players were tested for the precision of actions with the ball.

Thorough blood test confirmed that physiological changes after performing the first and the second task resembled. The precision of actions with the ball comparing to the initial level of all players increased after the familiar load and decreased after non-football load though (see the annex to chapter and table 2).

In another experiment players were suggested to perform two tasks, each of which should surely induce various physiological changes in the body, but both tasks consisted of football drills familiar for players. Before and after performing tasks players were tested for the precision of actions with the ball.

Table 2. Change in precision of players' actions with the ball comparing to the initial level after performing specific and nonspecific tasks, induced the same physiological changes in the body

After familiar (football) drills	After unfamiliar (non-football) drills
improvement in results	**deterioration in results**

Physiological changes occurred in the players' body after each task were indeed different, though the precision of actions with the ball increased for all players comparing to the initial level roughly to the same extent after performing the first and the second tasks either (table 3).

Table 3. Change in precision of players' actions with the ball comparing to the initial level after performing specific tasks, induced different physiological changes in the body

After drills induced insignificant physiological changes	After drills induced significant physiological changes
improvement in results	**improvement in results**

If drills induce physiological changes familiar for players, the precision of actions with the ball is defined not with a magnitude of these changes, but mostly with a nature of performed drills in the context of motor actions specificity.

Therefore the specificity of a certain load should be considered wherever from the physiological point of view, because while performing some work players are in a certain fitness shape, or from the biomechanical one, because performed actions may be different in nature (specific and nonspecific).

In the context of a value of physiological impact made and nature of performed movements training drills, which are used in football, may be combined into certain groups. Researches with participation of players from several teams were conducted to find out how such drills impact on the quality of actions with the ball.

Players were suggested to perform three kinds of tasks.

Each kind of tasks included specific and nonspecific drills, with, while performing drills of the first kind, players should act with a low and medium output necessarily, the second kind – with a high output, and the third – with an ultimate one.

Physiological impact of specific and nonspecific drills of the same output was nearly the same, as these drills were same on intensity, duration, work and rest intervals.

The impact of performed drills on the quality of actions with the ball (precision of shots on goal and passes with a mounted trajectory, speed and precision of dribbling) has been assessed.

Due to the fact that changes in the quality of players' performance of various actions with the ball turned out to be completely similar, they may be considered in a generalized form.

We should emphasize once again that results of these researches bear evidence of impact which different on specificity and physiological focus drills have on change in quality of players' actions with the ball during and directly after performing these drills only.

All specific drills result in positive changes in quality of actions with the ball, while unspecific (excluding drills with low and medium output) – in negative ones. The degree of impact (both negative and positive) is different in dependence to power of actions drills are performed with (fig. 17).

Specific drills with a high power of actions have the most significant positive impact on the quality of actions with the ball.

Contrarily, nonspecific drills with a high power of actions are related with the most significant negative changes in precision (quickness and precision) of techniques performance.

Sufficient positive impact of specific drills with a high power of actions on the quality of players handling the ball on course of researches may be explained by the fact that these drills virtually simulated drills that performed by players in trainings most often.

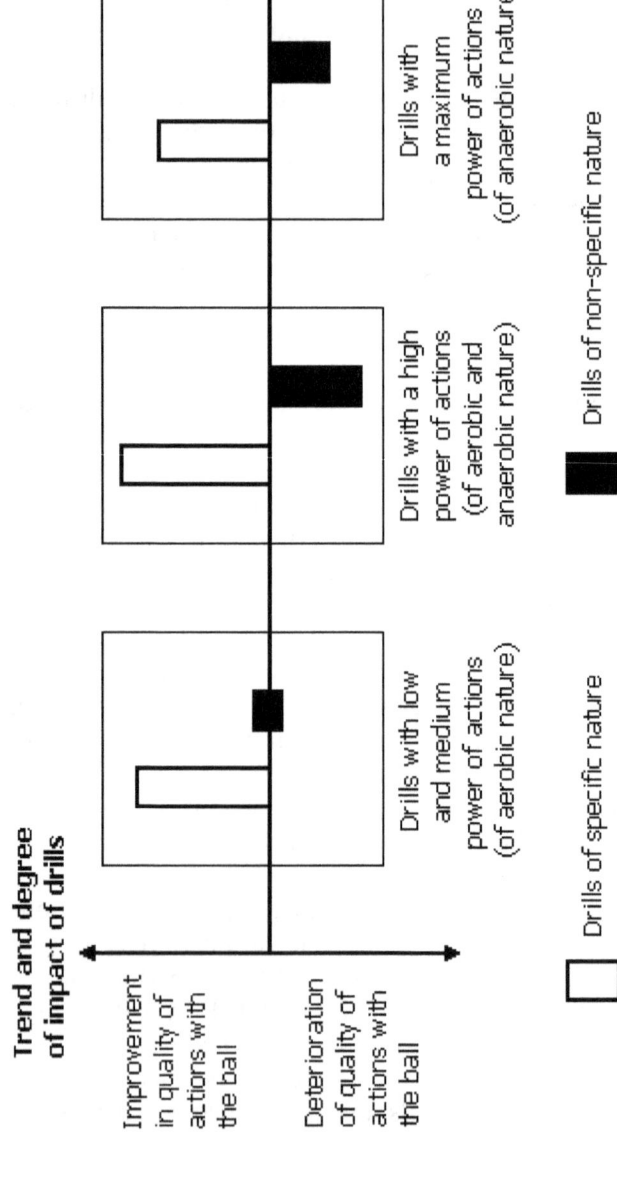

Fig. 17. Integrated specifications of the degree of impact of specific and nonspecific drills of different physiological focus on the quality (quickness and precision) of players' actions with the ball (following dispersion analysis)

It is also necessary to note that specific drills with a maximum power of actions caused the biggest changes in the quality of handling the ball in forwards, i. e. those who have to act with the ball most powerfully in trainings and games most often.

Working load may result either in positive and negative changes in the quality of players' actions with the ball. Whether these changes are positive or negative, and also the amount of these changes, is determined by players' habitualness to a certain load in the context of physiological changes occurred in the body and by the type of this load in the context of motor actions specificity.

Psychic impact

Increasing the responsibility for the effect of action

The game in various areas of the pitch is related with a various degree of responsibility. The higher responsibility for the effect of actions, the stronger mental impact it has on players. For example, some very skilled players admitted that felt uncomfortably, when get into opponents' 18-yard box during competitive matches.

Enormous responsibility falls particularly on players performing penalty kicks, and even the world's best players sometimes fail to convert such shots.

If a penalty kick isn't scored, it means that a shot was too weak or the ball was sent inaccurately. In any case player's movements were not precise because of a strong mental impact he faces.

Though not all players decrease the precision of actions with the ball in conditions, unfamiliar in the context of mental health. There are players who perform techniques as always in such situations, while some of them even discover reserves for increasing of the precision of actions with the ball (fig. 18).

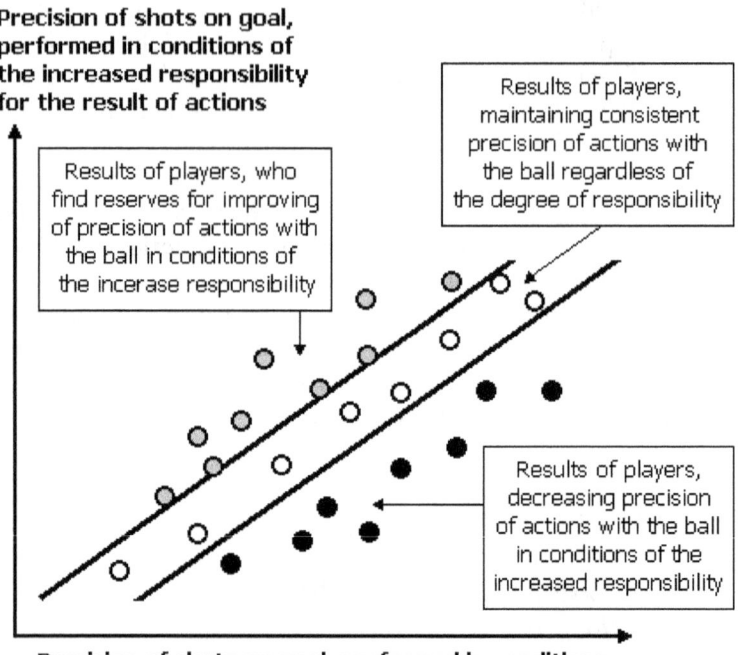

There is a relation between the indicators of the precision of actions with the ball, displayed by certain players in conditions of increased responsibility for the result and without it: generally players more prepared technically handle the ball more accurately in both cases.

A slight degree of connection shows that while increasing the responsibility for the result of actions some players discover reserves for increasing of the precision of actions with the ball, others maintain it, and still others decrease the precision

Fig. 18. Correlation of accuracy figures of shots on goal performed by players in conditions of various degree of responsibility for the result

Decrease in the precision of actions with the ball for certain players in unfamiliar conditions of increased responsibility for the result is explained with three reasons:
– a sharp increase in activity of antagonistic muscles;
– a spontaneous increase of duration of a movement pre-realization phase;
– lower speed of a striking link movement before touching the ball comparing to cases when techniques are performed without certain responsibility for their result.

The reduction in the quality of actions with the ball, when demands for precision of techniques performance are increased, for example by reducing the size of the goal area, where player should send the ball, is explained with the same reasons.

Players get used to strong mental impacts also differently: some very quickly, others a bit slowly, while still others cannot get used at all.

In this case adjustment is particularly gaining experience of performing actions with the ball in corresponding mental conditions, experience of participation in competition of a highest mental tension. It is impossible to create such conditions in training.

Making decision on action

In various game episodes player may choose decision how to act differently:
– deliberately, when he decides what to do in advance;
– on impulse, if he couldn't predefine what to do, and acts ad hoc;
– deliberately or on impulse, when one variant of actions is selected of two or three prepared ones depending on the scenario on the pitch.

The precision of techniques performance largely depends on how the making decision on actions is going on. Results of the following experiment may lend evidence for this.

After receiving the ball players were suggested to shoot on goal with a second touch, trying to send the ball:

— in the first task — into pre-specified area of the goal regardless of the goalkeeper's behavior;

— in the second task — into area of the goal most «favorable» to score.

Registration of motions of calf and foot of a striking leg with special footage has revealed that shooting technique differs in the first and second tasks (table 4).

With formal resemblance of player's movements with the ball, acting deliberately or on impulse, the inner organization of his movements is not similar in these cases.

If players decide which action with the ball would be performed in advance, they have more chances to show the higher precision.

Regardless of method of making decision how to act, players decrease the precision of actions with the ball when get in situations unfamiliar for them in the context of psychic atmosphere.

Once such situations become more or less familiar for them after several trainings, though, there is no decrease in the precision of techniques performance in these conditions.

Certain objectives

If a player performs a task responsibly all the time, he may display different precision of actions with the ball depending on what he is aimed at. Results of the following experiments may be lend evidence for this.

Skilled players were suggested to perform three sets of shots with a foot from 16 meters with sending the ball on target, with players were given prescription to perform shots:

— in the first set — with a maximum power necessarily;

— in the second set — in a most comfortable and familiar way;

— in the third set — so that the ball doesn't fly off the target after any shot.

Table 4. The distinctive features of players' performing shots on goal with a second touch with deliberate and deliberately-impulsive actions (on dynamic indicators of speed-ups of kicking leg links

Movements of links of striking leg	Actions of player'	Phases of motor action	
		Preparative (from the moment of a first touching the ball till the beginning of a striking motion)	Striking motion itself (from the beginning of a strike motion till the moment of touching the ball)
foot	deliberate	smooth movements with a constant speed-up	smooth increase of a speed-up towards with reaching the maximum **in the last third** of a strike motion
foot	deliberately-impulsive	disordered change of speed-ups in three planes	sharp increase of a speed-up towards **in the first third** of a striking motion
calf	deliberate	disordered change of speed-ups in three planes	sharp increase of a speed-up towards **in the first third** of a striking motion
calf	deliberately-impulsive	smooth movement with a constant speed-up	smooth increase of a speed-up towards with reaching the maximum **in the last third** of a strike motion

Seemingly players should display the highest precision while performing shots in the third set, when the task was to shoot with a maximum precision. But players sent the ball off the target most often exactly while performing the third set of shots, and they tried to shoot with a little power as a rule.

Players were most precise while performing the second set of shots, when it was not required to necessarily display just maximum power or just maximum precision of shots, and they could shoot in the most comfortable way.

When in another experiment players were suggested to perform the same actions with the ball either with a maximum speed or maximum precision, or quickly and precisely at the same time, players displayed different result in these cases, performing the task responsibly.

Depending on what they are aimed at, different precision of players performing the same actions with the ball is explained with the following: various certain objectives impact on the players' structure of movements at the last (fig. 19).

Use of psychostimulants

After receiving psychostimulants players usually begin to act with increased intensity.

If players use these pharmacologicals for the first time, they go into unfamiliar mental state, and it remains to be seen how does it impact on the precision of their actions with the ball.

In these cases no one generally displays enduring accuracy in performing techniques, because the ball simply stops to «respond» to players in state of excitement, yet in certain episodes some of the players may essentially show the highest skill in handling the ball.

In the context of reaching the enduring accuracy in actions with the ball there is no point to reckon on the positive effect after players receiving psychostimulants for the first time. Players would handle the ball precisely in case the impact these psychostimulants have becomes familiar for them.

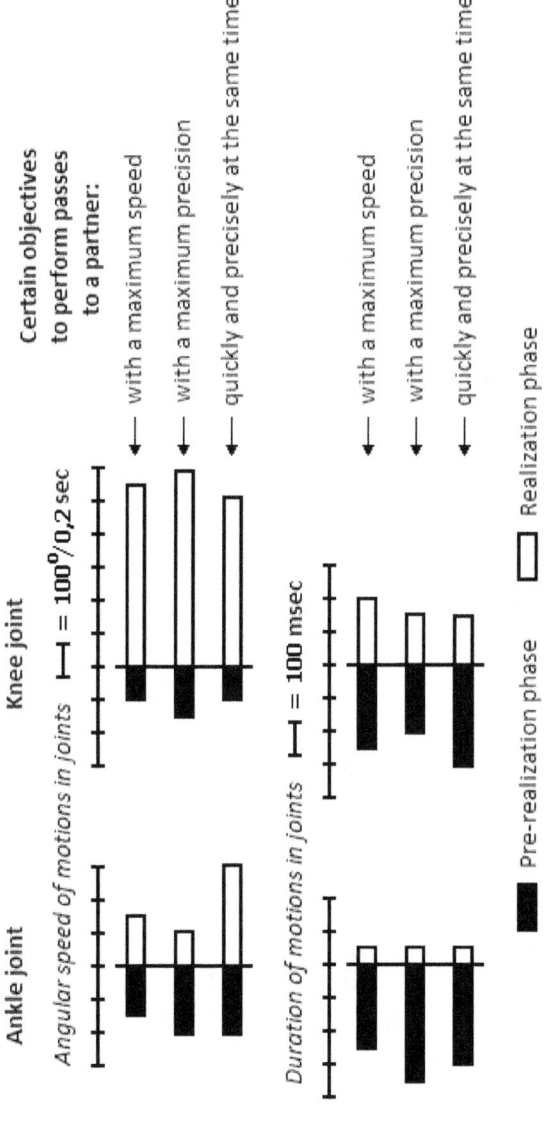

Fig. 19. Kinematic characteristics of players' movements while performing passes to a partner with a mounted trajectory with various certain objectives (on indicators of angular speed and duration of motions in joints)

It is possible to achieve addiction to the effects of certain psychostimulants with its regular use, **though it is dangerous to players' health.** There were cases when high class players have been taking psychostimulants consistently before competitive matches for 20-25 times. They had to end their sporting career earlier, and all of them had their health ruined.

Speed of moving, tempo and mode of players' movements

If players aren't used to handle the ball while running with a maximum speed, they decrease the precision of actions with the ball abruptly, when it is necessary to act at the breaking point of own speed capabilities in the game.

This is due to the fact that while moving at a great speed players prepare to contact and contact with the ball differently than while running with a lower speed, as there occur changes in speed of certain body parts movements, running tempo, efforts while repulsion off the ground and while touching the ball. Therefore it is no coincidence that in football they outline so called «high speed technique».

Generally the precision of handling the ball may worsen not only when it is necessary to act at unfamiliar higher speed, but also in cases when sportsmen used to play only at a maximum speed switch to a lower speed unfamiliar for them.

In football switch to a game with a lower speed doesn't result in increasing of technical defects, because actions with the ball at such speed are familiar to all players. In some kinds of sport though, when sportsmen get in easier conditions comparing to those they got used to play and train in, the decrease in the precision of movements appears brightly enough.

For example, hockey players, bound to act at a high speed and in permanent contact with an opponent, note that during the penalty shootout, when there is no chasing opponent and it is possible to move with a lower speed, when nobody pushes and holds them down, they feel less confident, than while going one on one with the goalkeeper during the game.

Experienced hockey players therefore try to perform penalty shot moving at a maximum speed from the beginning till the end.

While performing certain actions with the ball or a set of techniques (dribbling, dummies, first touches with following shot on goal), players observe certain chronological sequence of various body parts movements – movements tempo.

The precision of actions with the ball is the highest when players act in familiar tempo. Going beyond the familiar tempo results in increasing of technical defects.

It is hard to point out the relation between movement tempo and the precision of techniques performance in football visually, but in other sports it is seen clearly enough.

For example, in tennis and ping-pong each sportsman has his own tempo of play (frequency of consecutive strikes while playing the ball) he reaches his maximum precision of strikes with. Any deviations from the familiar tempo (either increasing or lowering) result in losses in the precision of movements. As a rule, in tennis the one who is able to impose his tempo to the opponent wins of two nearly equal opponents.

Sometimes in training players are suggested before handling the ball to perform such movements (or a set of movements), which they never perform in game directly before performing techniques. This may be, for example, a roll over (a set of roll overs) or jumps over obstacles before shooting on goal. It is generally thought that the agility of movements is developed in such a way.

Though after such movements the precision of actions with the ball performed directly after decays. And in case players in training would constantly rollover before shooting on goal, when bunch of movements «roll over and shot on goal» becomes familiar for them, and in games shots on goal would be precise in cases when players get in time to roll over before the shot.

Therefore it is necessary for skilled players to train movements and bunches of movements that occur in competitive games, while the agility and physical coordination should be developed at young players' early age.

Impacts on motor sensitivity

Any impacts on the joint sensitivity through which the course of strike motions is controlled always affect (positively or negatively) the precision of actions with the ball.

Complete «switching off» of the joint sensitivity, for example by means of special anesthetic techniques, results in such incoordination of human movements that it is impossible to talk about some intentional movement performance.

A wide variety of factors may affect the joint sensitivity and the precision of players' actions with the ball subsequently.

Strength exercises

Heavy load exercises, which have heavy strength influence (uncharacteristic for football) on leg muscles and joints, affect the precision of techniques, performed directly after and requiring differentiation of efforts, negatively. After such exercises players just lose the «ball feel» for some time.

In case during the long period of time players would train actions with the ball requiring delicate differentiation of efforts directly after heavy strength influence, then undesired skills are imprinted.

Using balls of different weight and size

The lighter the ball, the higher degree of sensory acuity is required from players for precise techniques performance.

When players handle the lightweight ball (comparing to the ball of a usual weight) for a while, all existing reserves of motor sensitivity are involved. In case actions with the ball of a usual weight are performed right afterwards, we may observe the increase in the precision of techniques performance.

Certain increase in the precision of actions with the standard ball also occurs after using the ball of smaller size.

If players are suggested to handle the weighted ball, the precision of actions with the standard ball decreases after that.

Any change in the ball characteristics not only affects the motor sensitivity, but also results in disruption of players' movements naturalness (fig. 20).

It is evident even for an eye that efforts of calf and foot, as with the standard ball, are not enough to contact with the ball for a player performing a dribbling with the weighted ball, and other muscle groups are also involved into work.

When players act with lightweight and smaller balls, their movements also differ from movements apparent while handling the ball of a standard weight.

If balls of irregular weight and size are used in training consistently and over a long period of time, unnatural for football movements would be imprinted.

Physical impact

Physical contact with the opponent

It makes no sense to describe in detail what is so obvious: direct physical contact of a player possessing the ball with an opponent commonly results in disruption of forms of motion and decreasing of precision of actions with the ball as a result.

In some cases contact interaction may seemingly not impact players' movements, but ongoing changes in «inner» organization of movements may result in lowering of quality of actions with the ball.

Amid touch duels players, for whom such game is obviously unfamiliar, begin to make much more mistakes. If it is usual for a player to play in contact with an opponent, he may demonstrate the enduring accuracy in actions with the ball even in these cases.

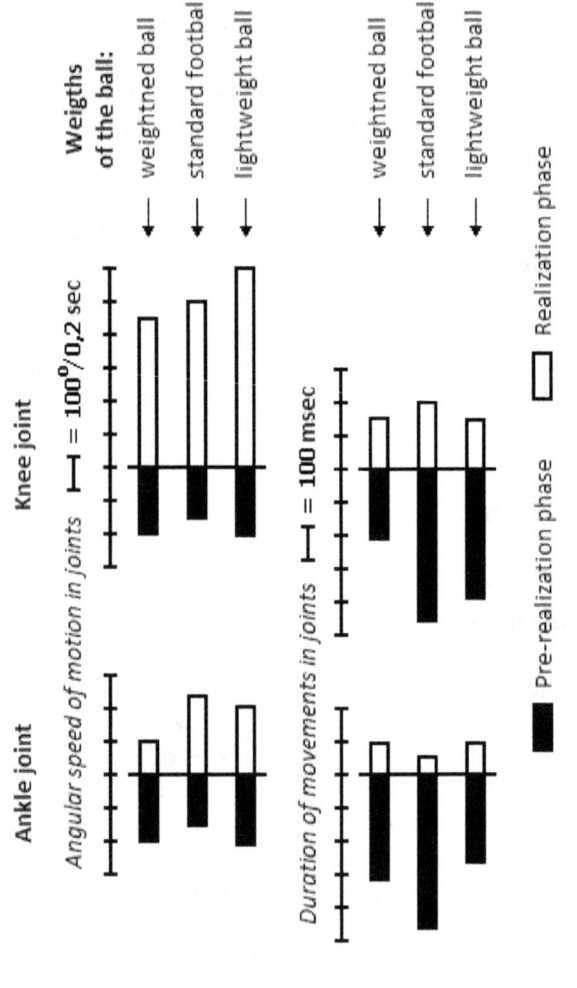

Players' structure of movements changes dramatically while performing actions with the ball which weight differ markedly from the standard ball

Fig. 20. Kinematic characteristics of players' movements while performing dribbling with the ball of a different weight (on indicators of angular speed and duration of motions in joints)

Use of additional technical and mechanical facilities

Any physical impacts on players, related to use of various additional technical and mechanical facilities, including any and all weighting for various body parts (blades, belts, special shoes), cause disturbances in natural for football coordination of muscle work, developed sequence of certain body parts kicking into gear and result in lowering of quality of actions with the ball (fig. 21).

Longstanding employment of facilities, affecting the players' movements naturalness, result in destruction of motor programs of actions with the ball, largely developed earlier.

Negative impact such facilities have on the precision of players' actions affects for a while after stop of their use.

Attempts to use various weightings while perfecting technical skills were also undertaken in other sports.

For example, while training technical skills on ice hockey players used not only weighted belts, but also weighted bandies and pucks, and sometimes tied an additional load to themselves (weight plates from 10 to 20 kilos). In the end they have abandon all of this, as such tasks affect negatively (as evidenced by experiments) hockey players' speed of movement, their shots power and precision.

At some point boxers trained for a long time with weightings, holding them in hands, to increase the striking power. In all cases this resulted in losing the quickness and precision of movements and accented punch. Therefore in boxing they have abandoned such exercises.

Massage

What is meant here is the massage directly before the training or game. Such massage may have different impact on the precision of players' actions with the ball depending on its focus and nature, to a greater or lesser extent for different players.

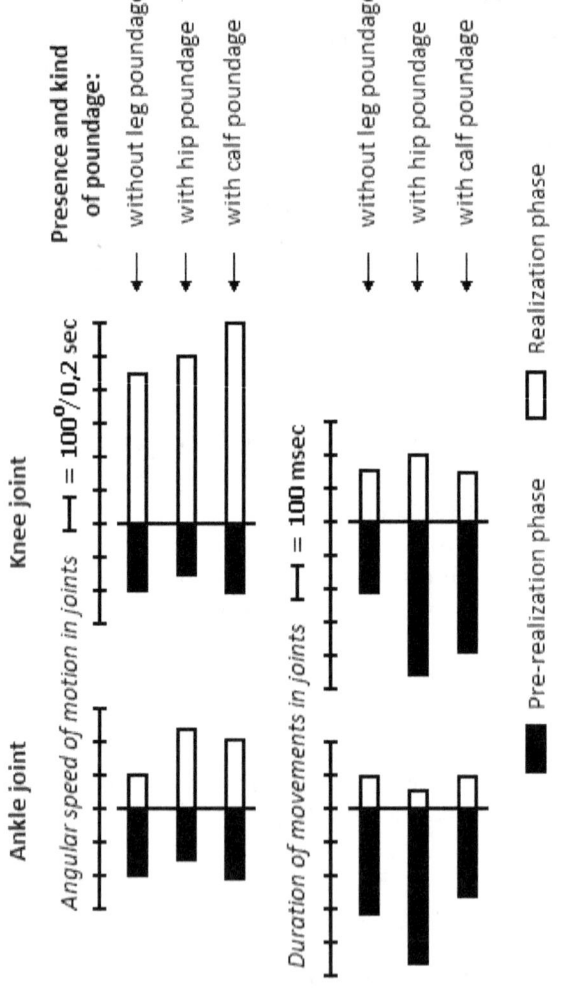

Fig. 21. Kinematic characteristics of players' movements while performing a dribbling with or without leg poundage (on indicators of angular speed and duration of motions in joints)

Deep intense muscle massage has considerable impact on muscles' «well-being», and, depending on the frequency of its use, may result in a player getting into the familiar or unfamiliar state. If deep muscle massage is performed occasionally, it would negatively affect this player's precision of actions with the ball for a while.

Contrarily, thorough massage of leg joints enhances the precision of actions with the ball performed by players afterwards, though such impact intervenes for 10-15 minutes.

Pitch surface

Pitch surface is another factor able to have a specific impact on quality of players' actions with the ball.

Transition from familiar surface to unfamiliar always makes players feel uncomfortable. If there is transition to a surface different from a natural with its elastic characteristics, this is not only due to the decrease in the precision of players handling the ball, but also to the increasing of probability of getting injured.

Starting time of training throughout the day

One of the factors that may affect the precision of players' actions with the ball is time. We mean not only time on which a player may have a lead over an opponent in play episode, but also time in a broader sense.

In some degree the players' body is sensitive to the starting time of training throughout the day, to the game duration, to time between games and even to time of substitutions.

Starting time of training throughout the day is related to the precision of actions with the ball, which is confirmed by results of the following experiment.

Players from non-professional and professional teams, while being at recovering camp without training, were suggested to perform shots on goal and passes with a mounted trajectory into a horizontal target each hour throughout the day.

It emerged that the precision of players' performance of shots on goal and passes had been varied throughout the day, but players acted with the ball most precisely exactly at the time they used to train (fig. 22).

Players from non-professional team, accustomed to consistently train once a day in evening, have demonstrated their best result at the same time.

Two peaks of the increasing in the precision of actions with the ball, coinciding with the time of daily training, were observed in professional players performing daily trainings twice a day over lengthy periods of time.

All players performed techniques with the lowest precision at dinner-time regardless of qualification.

Results of this experiment show that the habitualness to the certain load, determining the precision of players' actions with the ball, consists of players' habitualness not only to training and game conditions directly, but also to their timing.

Resume

Research results represented in this chapter show that various external factors may either positively or negatively affect on the quality of players actions with the ball.

The amount and nature of change in precision (quickness and precision) of techniques performance under influence of the certain impact are defined with the following main provision: does player have or have not a subjective previous experience of facing such impact in practice.

Whether failures in realization of motor programs of actions with the ball would occur, and if yes then of what dimension, depends exactly on the extent of players' habitualness to the impact of one or another factor.

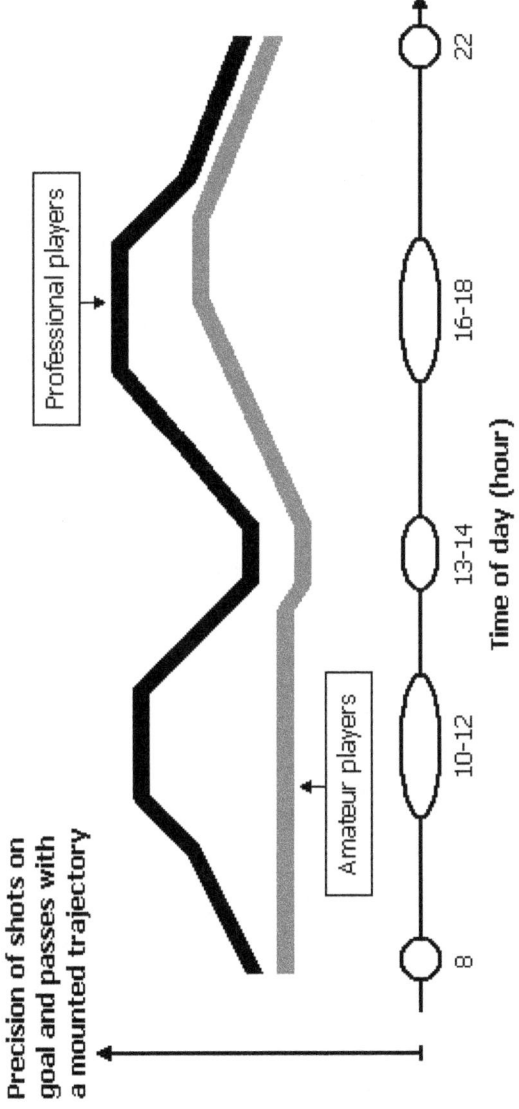

Players demonstrate the highest precision of actions with the ball at the time of day when they usually train

Fig. 22. The dynamics of the precision of shots on goal and passes with a mounted trajectory while performing such actions by players of different qualification at different times of day in recovery camp (in period when there are no intentional trainings)

From this perspective the most important in training for skilled players while perfecting the technical prowess is to:

– ensure that impacts they may meet in competitive games would become familiar for them;

– avoid those impacts which may result in consolidation of undesired motor skills while handling the ball.

Enclosure

Impact of specific and non-specific load, induced the same physiological changes in the body, on the precision of players shooting on target with a foot

	Biochemical values of blood after getting a load		
	specific	non-specific	
PH	7,238	7,229	In biochemical values of blood after getting specific and non-specific loads there were no statistically significant differences
pCO_2	38,0	37,45	
pO_2	68,37	69,55	
HCO_2	17,15	16,63	
CO_2	18,62	17,69	
BE	-8,68	-9,02	
SB	17,73	17,2	

	Indicators of precision of shots (cm) after getting a load		Impact of the load specificity (on analysis of variance)
	specific	non-specific	
X (average bias of the ball deviations in vertical direction)	7,0	12,8	18,5%
Y (average bias of the ball deviations in horizontal direction)	1,83	5,72	14,8%
Gx (density of points of impact in vertical direction)	35,9	40,3	6,8%
Gy (density of points of impact in horizontal direction)	25,1	30,6	6,6%

The dynamics of kinematic characteristics of players' movements while performing shots on goal with a foot for a long period of time (average data and indicators variability for every 100 attempts to perform a shot by the test player)

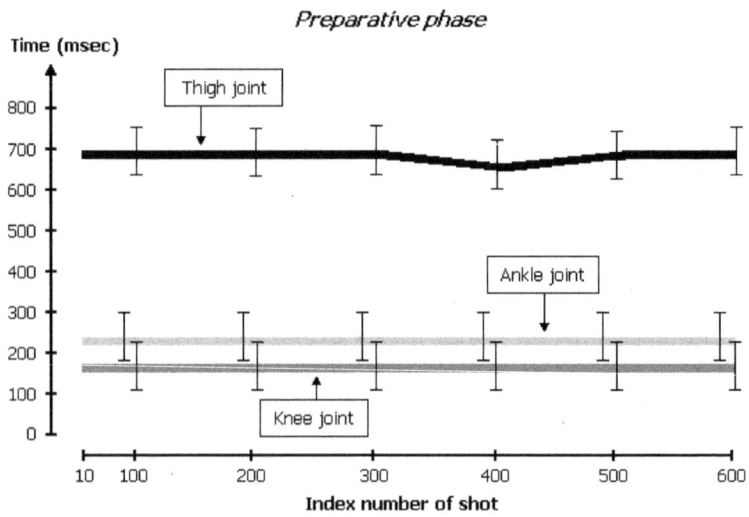

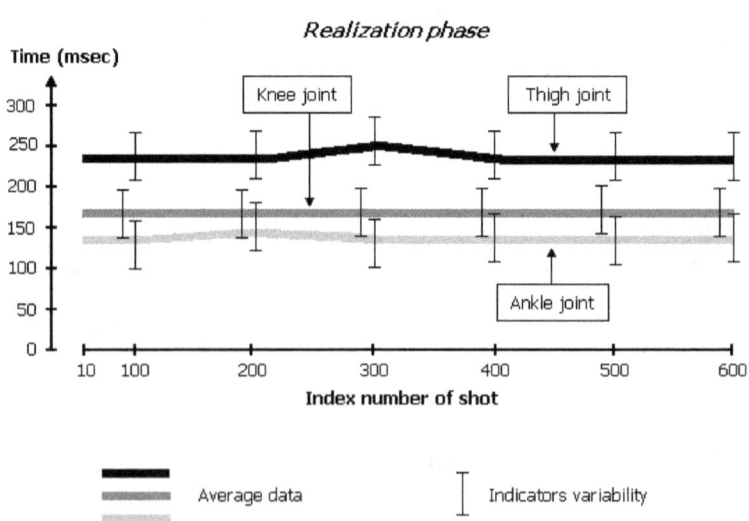

Football. Theory of training of speed and precision of actions with the ball by players

For notes

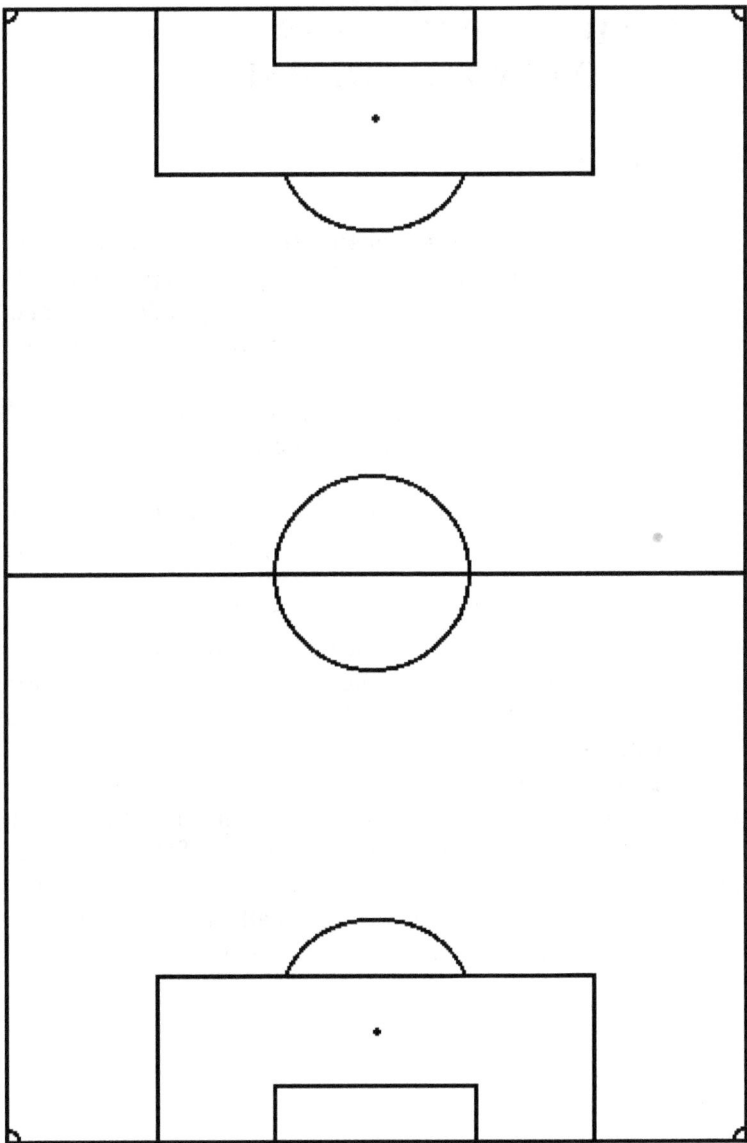

CHAPTER 4.
TRANSITION OF FITNESS IN SPEED AND PRECISION OF ACTIONS WITH THE BALL

Introduction

The facts show that the quality (quickness and precision) of performing techniques by skilled players depends on the conditions players are in: in familiar, fitting into developed earlier motor programs of actions with the ball, or in unfamiliar, drawing out of these programs.

Do players improve exactly those actions with the ball in training, which they have to perform in competitive matches?

This poses a question on the transition of fitness in speed and precision of actions with the ball while moving from training conditions to conditions of competitive games.

It is hard to define in practical work which drill brings positive results and which is useless. Long-term studies, which results are presented in this chapter, were conducted to explore the phenomenon of fitness transition in speed and precision of actions with the ball.

Terms **«transition of fitness»** and **«transition of speed and precision»** will be used while presenting the material. In this book they would mean the transition of fitness in the precision (quickness and precision) of movements, when it is necessary to perform actions with the ball in conditions differ from those in which these actions was trained.

The concept of fitness transition

The efficiency of drills used by skilled players is entirely measured with whether they allow to improve results in competitions or, in other words, if there is the transition of fitness from the training conditions to competitive.

The essence of sport training is in reaching the transition of fitness. In this regard the phenomenon of fitness transition exactly shows, what, when and how much should skilled players do in training, and determines the choice of certain drills.

If some drill doesn't allow to improve competitive results, when in these cases we may talk of absence of fitness transition and that this drill is useless and time was wasted.

Some drills may not only not provide positive developments, but even affect players' actions negatively briefly after, i. e. **result in negative fitness transition.**

Sometimes practical work suggests that physiological, biomechanical and mental impacts of some drills may be negative and cause deterioration in players' competitive results, though it is necessary to have a big experience and spend a lot of time to finally make it certain. Therefore in many cases it is still not fully understood that players' unsuccessful actions in competitive games are directly linked with the use of certain drills.

The phenomenon of fitness transition, both positive and negative, suggests reaching of accumulative effect as a result of applying of certain drills during the relatively long period of time, and not getting immediate developments (immediate training effect) right after performing one or another drill.

Certain drill may have positive or negative immediate effect, but it doesn't mean that the same positive or negative effect would occur with prolonged application of this drill.

Fitness transition while perfecting the precision in performance of techniques and developing motor characteristics and functional capabilities happens differently on principle.

Fundamentals of transition of fitness in the precision of actions with the ball

There is an opinion that there is fitness transition from one conditions to another while training functional systems (vascular and respiratory), providing the sportsmen body with an oxygen.

The work of these systems may be improved by means of various motor tasks, for example usual run, skiing, swimming or sport games, if these tasks are performed in modes allowing to develop capabilities of cardiac muscle and respiratory system.

Regardless of drills by which this was achieved, well-trained heart and respiratory system allow to durably perform football tasks with low and medium intensity.

But can we say that fitness transition in the precision of interaction with the ball is going on exactly in the same manner, as during the transition from one conditions of techniques performance to another?

Results of experiments conducted in football and other sport games, in which the impact of various drills on changes in the quality of performance of actions with the ball was considered, allowed to note the following.

Positive developments in the precision (quickness and precision) of techniques performance by skilled players were observed only in cases when players were in familiar conditions, i. e. when conditions of performance of actions with the ball in test tasks coincided with conditions of drills that had been used in trainings earlier, either in the context of physiological impact on the body and nature of motor actions.

Researches in football were arranged to examine this proposition, in which it was considered how the transition of fitness happens in the precision (quickness and precision) of techniques performance by players, when it is necessary to perform actions with the ball in conditions differ from those, in which the same actions were trained, specifically if changed are:

– the quickness of techniques performance and value of efforts applied by players to perform actions with the ball, and also the external shape of movements with the ball (kinematic and dynamic characteristics);

– players' fitness shape as a while and leg muscles condition by the time of performing actions with the ball under various working loads (global or local);

– requirements for visual perception and displaying of motor sensitivity.

Undertaken studies allowed to enunciate the following fundamentals of fitness transition in the quickness and precision of actions with the ball.

First. If players were training actions with the ball in one conditions (in the context of quickness of skills performance, efforts applied by players for this performance, external shape of motor actions), while it is necessary to perform these actions in other conditions, there is **no transition** of precision (quickness and precision).

Second. If players were training actions with the ball in one conditions (in the context of players' fitness shape, leg muscle condition at the moment of techniques performance), while it is necessary to perform these actions in other conditions, there is **no transition** of precision (quickness and precision).

Third. If players were training actions with the ball in more simple conditions (in the context of requirements for visual perception and displaying of motor sensitivity), while it is necessary to perform these actions in other conditions, there is **no transition** of precision (quickness and precision).

Fourth. If players were training actions with the ball in more complicated conditions (in the context of requirements for visual perception and displaying of motor sensitivity), while it is necessary to perform these actions in more simple conditions, there is **a transition** of precision (quickness and precision).

Following are the description and results of experiments, each of which lasted for 1,5-2 months. In this time players trained for 20-25 times.

In all experiments players were divided into groups, in which they trained actions with the ball in certain given conditions. Before and after experiments players were tested for the precision of shots on goal, passes with a mounted trajectory, speed and precision of dribbling in conditions, which they trained and didn't train these techniques in. The impact of experimental trainings on the quality of these actions with the ball in either conditions was assessed.

We should emphasize, that the goal of these researches was no to find out whether players would play better or worse, but to educe the presence or absence of fitness transition in quickness and precision of actions with the ball after using different training drills during the long period of time.

Fitness transition while training shots on goal

The transition in fitness while training of shots on goal with a foot was considered for cases when there were changes in power and distance of shots, trajectory of the ball, position of the ball before the shot (on the pitch surface or at some height above it), direction of player's movements with the ball relative to the goal before the shots and body shape relative to the direction of sending the ball at the moment of shot.

During the experiment players have been performing following tasks.

Tasks performed by players from different groups in experimental trainings	Features characterizing tasks
In the 1st group: shots with a maximum power **In the 2nd group:** shots from the same distance with a medium power	power of shooting
In the 1st group: shots with a maximum power from 16 meters **In the 2nd group:** shots with a maximum power from 25 meters	distance of shooting

In the 1st group: shots from 20 meters with sending the ball with a trajectory close to linear **In the 2nd group:** shots from 20 meters with sending the ball with an embowed trajectory with a sidespin of the ball	trajectory of sending the ball
In the 1st group: shots from the position opposite to the goal face to it after fast dribbling (fig. A) **In the 2nd group:** shots from the same distance from position at angle to the goal sideways to it after fast dribbling (fig. B) *[diagram showing positions A and B relative to goals]*	direction of player's movement with the ball relative to the goal before shooting and his body shape relative to the direction of sending the ball at the moment of shooting
In the 1st group: kicks on the ball positioned on the pitch surface **In the 2nd group:** shots from the same distance on the ball positioned at some height above the pitch surface (bouncing off the pitch)	position of the ball at the moment of shooting

Results of experimental trainings have revealed the following:

– players, who have been training shots on goal with a maximum power, have improved the precision of shots performed exactly with a maximum power;

– players, who have been training shots on goal with a medium power, have improved the precision of shots performed exactly with a medium power (table 5).

Table 5. Comparison of results demonstrated by players who have been training shots on goal with a foot from the same distance, but with different power, while performing the same test tasks before and after the experiment

Test tasks	
shooting on goal with a maximum power	shooting on goal with a medium power
In the 1st group: improvement in results	In the 1st group: no change in results
In the 2nd group: no change in results	In the 2nd group: improvement in results

If players have been training shots on goal with a certain power, while it is necessary to perform shots on goal from the same distance with another power, there is no fitness transition.

Results of experimental trainings have revealed the following:

– players, who have been training shots on goal from 16 meters with a maximum power, have improved the precision of shots performed with a maximum power exactly from 16 meters;

– players, who have been training shots on goal from 25 meters with a maximum power, have improved the precision of shots performed with a maximum power from 25 and 16 meters either (table 6).

Absence or presence of changes in the precision of players performing shots on goal with a maximum power in test tasks is explained with the following.

Players who have been training shots on goal with a maximum power from 16 meters during the experiment, have developed a certain angle of sending the ball (have consolidated certain moves of supporting and kicking legs, body position), which is necessary to hold out to send the ball not above the bar with a maximum power exactly from this distance.

Table 6. Comparison of results demonstrated by players who have been training shots on goal with a foot with a maximum power, but from different distances, while performing the same test tasks before and after the experiment

Test tasks	
shots on goal from 16 meters with a maximum power	shots on goal from 25 meters with a maximum power
In the 1st group: improvement in results	In the 1st group: no change in results
In the 2nd group: improvement in results	In the 2nd group: improvement in results

When in test task these players have been performing shots with a maximum power from 25 meters, they spontaneously keep an angle of sending the ball, consolidated during the training, that prevented them from improving the initial level of the precision of shots from 25 meters.

Players who have been performing shots on goal from 25 meters also have consolidated certain yet slightly smaller angle of the ball's flight, necessary for the ball to precisely hit the target while performing shots with a maximum power exactly from this distance. Performing shots with a maximum power from 16 meters in a test task, these players have been sending the ball with the angle of sending, consolidated during the experimental trainings, with which the ball couldn't fly above the bar. This allowed them to improve also the initial level of the precision of shots with a maximum power from 16 meters (fig. 23).

Players who have been training shots on goal with a maximum power from long distances may demonstrate good results while performing shots with the same power and from closer distances. Players who have been training shots on goal with a maximum power from close distances send the ball above the bar while performing shots with the same power from a longer distance, maintaining the angle of sending the ball, consolidated in trainings.

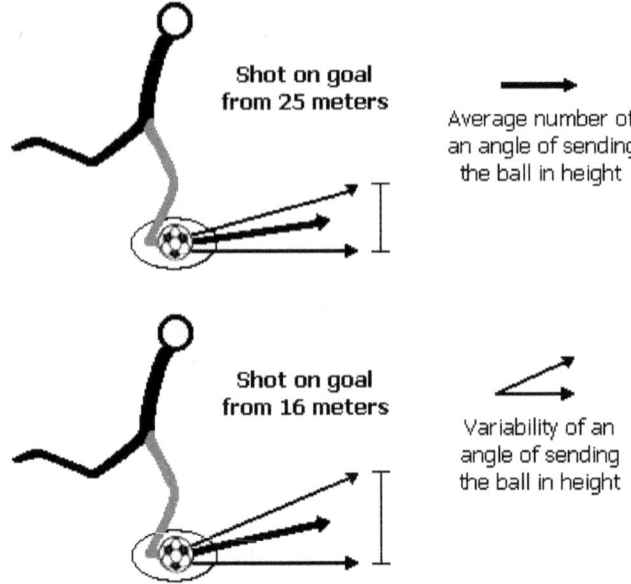

Fig. 23. Angle of sending the ball in height (average numbers and variability), consolidated during the training of shots on goal with a foot with a maximum power from different distances

Results of experimental trainings have revealed the following:
– players, who have been training shots on goal with sending the ball with a trajectory close to linear, have improved the precision of shots, performed exactly with sending the ball with a trajectory close to linear;
– players, who have been training shots on goal with sending the ball with an embowed trajectory with a sidespin of the ball, haven't improved the precision of shots, performed with sending the ball with a trajectory close to linear;
– only one player from four, who have been training shots on goal with sending the ball with an embowed trajectory with a sidespin of the ball, has improved the precision of such shots (table 7).

Table 7. Comparison of results demonstrated by players who have been training shots on goal with a foot from the same distance with different trajectory of sending the ball, while performing the same test tasks before and after the experiment

Test tasks	
shooting on goal with sending the ball with a trajectory close to linear	shooting on goal with sending the ball with an embowed trajectory with a sidespin
In the 1st group: **improvement in results**	In the 1st group: no change in results
In the 2nd group: no change in results	In the 2nd group: **improvement in results of certain players**

The fact that most players of those who have been training shots on goal with sending the ball with an embowed trajectory with a sidespin, failed to improve the quality of such shots performance, may be explained with the following.

These players have shooting skills with sending the ball with a trajectory close to linear so firmly consolidated it was very difficult for them to move to performing of curled shots, which are markedly different in the technique of performance.

If players have been training shots on goal with one trajectory of sending the ball (close to linear or embowed with a sidespin of the ball), while it is required to shoot on goal from the same distance with another one, there is no fitness transition.

Results of experimental trainings have revealed the following:

– players, who have been training shots on goal with the ball on the pitch surface, have improved the precision of exactly such shots;

– players, who have been training shots on goal with the ball at some height above the pitch surface (bouncing off the pitch), have improved the precision of exactly such shots (table 8).

Table 8. Comparison of results demonstrated by players who have been training shots on goal with a foot from the same distance with different position of the ball at the moment of shooting relative to the pitch surface, while performing the same test tasks before and after the experiment

Test tasks	
shooting on goal with the ball on the pitch surface	shooting on goal with the ball at some height above the pitch surface
In the 1st group: **improvement in results**	In the 1st group: no change in results
In the 2nd group: no change in results	In the 2nd group: **improvement in results**

If players have been training shots on goal with one position of the ball at the moment of shooting relative to the pitch surface, while it is required to perform shots on goal from the same distance with another position of the ball at the moment of shooting relative to the pitch surface, there is no fitness transition.

Results of experimental trainings have revealed the following:

– players, who have been training shots on goal opposite to the middle of the goal face to it, have improved the precision of shots performed exactly from such position;

– players, who have been training shots on goal from position at angle to the goal sideways to it, have improved the precision of shots performed exactly from such position (table 9).

Absence of fitness transition while performing shots on goal in test tasks in conditions players didn't train shots during the experiment, is explained by the fact that the supporting leg position, movements of the kicking leg and body movements while shooting from position at angle to the goal sideways to it differ from similar actions of players while performing shots from the position opposite to the middle of the goal face to it.

Table 9. Comparison of results demonstrated by players ho have been training shots on goal with a foot from the same distance with different directions of player's movements with the ball relative to the goal before shooting and his body positions relative to the direction of sending the ball at the moment of shooting, while performing the same test tasks before and after the experiment

Test tasks	
shooting on goal from the position opposite to the middle of the goal face to it	shooting on goal from the position at angle to the goal sideways to it
In the 1st group: **improvement in results**	In the 1st group: no change in results
In the 2nd group: no change in results	In the 2nd group: **improvement in results**

For players, who have been training shots on goal from position at angle to the goal sideways to it, it was difficult to maintain the speed of movements with the ball before the moment of kicking the ball.

Gradually they adjusted to uncomfortable conditions of shots performance, and also shot while diving in many cases, that didn't prevent them to demonstrate increasingly high precision.

If players have been training shots on goal with one direction of movement relative to the goal before shooting and body position relative to the direction of sending the ball at the moment of shooting, while it is required to shot on goal from the same distance in another direction of movements relative to the goal before shooting and body position relative to the direction of sending the ball at the moment of shooting, there is no fitness transition.

Fitness transition while training passes

The transition of fitness while training passes was considered for cases when the ball was sent:
– at long distance with a mounted trajectory;
– at medium distance across the pitch surface to the moving partner;
– at short distance across the pitch surface into the reflecting panel at some angle to the direction of passing player's movement (passes simulating one-two play).

During the experiment players have been performing following tasks.

Tasks performed by players from different groups during the experimental trainings
In the 1st group: moving with the ball at short distance with an average speed and a pass at 25 meters with a mounted trajectory on target marked on the pitch surface

In the 2nd group: moving with the ball at short distance with an average speed and a pass at 12-15 meters across the pitch surface to the moving partner so that he could receive the ball in the marked space without reducing the speed of movements
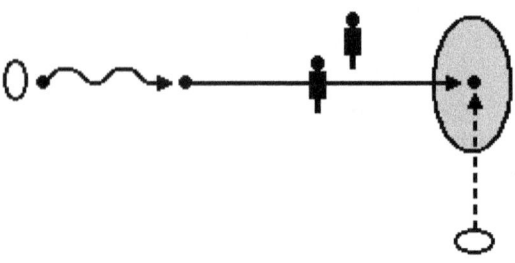

In the 3rd group: moving with the ball at short distance with an average speed and a pass at 4-5 meters across the pitch surface into the reflecting panel at angle to the direction of movement so that the ball bounces into the marked space, where player could receive the ball himself while running

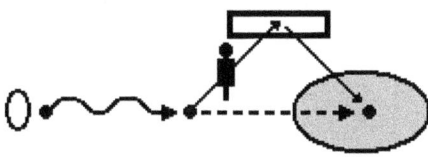

Results of experimental trainings have revealed the following:

– players, who have been training passes at long distance with a mounted trajectory, have improved the precision of passes exactly at long distance with a mounted trajectory;

– players, who have been training passes at average distance across the pitch surface to a moving partner, have improved the precision of passes exactly at average distance to a moving partner;

– players, who have been training passes at short distance across the pitch surface into the reflecting panel at some angle to the direction of movement, have insignificantly improved the precision of passes exactly at short distance across the pitch surface into the reflecting panel at some angle to the direction of movement (table 10).

The reason for insignificant increase in the precision of performance of passes at short distance by players, who have been training such passes, is that players have been performing it with significantly high precision from the beginning.

Absence of fitness transition while changing the distance and nature of passes is explained by the fact that in these cases different requirements to mechanisms of motor control, and coordination of muscles work differs as a result.

Table 10. Comparison of results demonstrated by players who have been training passes, different in technique of performance, while performing the sane tasks before and after the experiment

Test tasks		
movement with the ball at short distance with an average speed and a pass at 25 meters with a mounted trajectory into the target marked on the pitch surface	movement with the ball at short distance with an average speed and a pass at 12-15 meters across the pitch surface to a moving partner so that he could receive the ball in the marked space without reducing the speed of movement	movement with the ball at short distance with an average speed and a pass at 4-5 meters across the pitch surface into the reflecting panel at angle to the direction of movement so that the ball bounces into the marked space, where player could receive the ball himself while running
In the 1st group: **improvement of results**	In the 1st group: no change in results	In the 1st group: no change in results
In the 2nd group: no change in results	In the 2nd group: **improvement in results**	In the 2nd group: no change in results
In the 3rd group: no change in results	In the 3rd group: no change in results	In the 3rd group: **insignificant improvement in results**

While sending the ball into the reflecting panel it is required only to maintain the direction and figure out efforts, while passing to a moving partner it is also necessary to pass the ball timely, while performing passes with a mounted trajectory it is particularly important to choose the correct combination of an angle and speed of the ball's flight.

If players have been training certain passes (on distance and nature), while it is necessary to perform another, there is no fitness transition.

The transition of speed and precision while training the dribbling

The transition of speed and precision while training the dribbling was considered for cases when the dribbling at a maximum speed at short distance with change of the movement direction was performed with high and low requirements for precision of actions with the ball.

During the experiment players have been performing following tasks.

Tasks performed by players from different groups during the experimental trainings	
In the 1st group: the most fast and precise dribbling at 20 meters through five «goals» 0,5 meters wide	**In the 2nd group:** the most fast and precise dribbling at 20 meters through five «goals» 0,25 meters wide
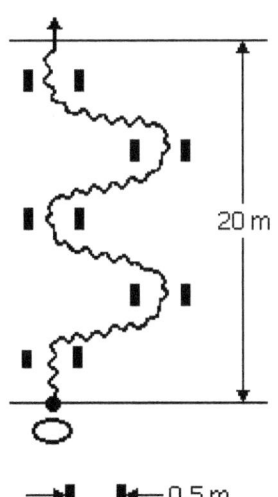	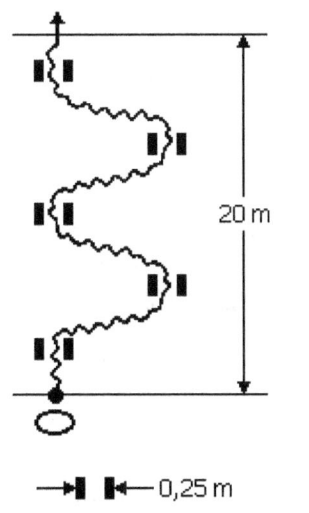
Note. «Goals» were marked on the pitch surface with a flat items not detaining the movement of the ball and a player	

Results of experimental trainings have revealed the following:

– players, who have been training the dribbling at a maximum speed with low requirements to the precision of actions (passing «goals» 0,5 meters wide), have improved results in dribbling exactly with low requirements to the movements precision;

– players, who have been training the dribbling at a maximum speed with high requirements to the precision of actions (passing «goals» 0,25 meters wide), have improved results in dribbling exactly with high requirements to the movements precision (table 11).

Table 11. Comparison of results demonstrated by players who have been training dribbling with change of the direction of movement with high and low requirements to the movements precision, while performing the same tasks before and after the experiment

Test tasks	
the most fast and precise dribbling at 20 meters through five «goals» 0,5 meters wide	the most fast and precise dribbling at 20 meters through five «goals» 0,25 meters wide
In the 1st group: **improvement in results**	In the 1st group: no change in results
In the 2nd group: no change in results	In the 2nd group: **improvement in results**

At first glance those players, who have been training dribbling in conditions, when requirements for the precision of actions performance were higher (with passing «goals» 0,25 meters wide), should also improve their results in dribbling, when requirements for the precision of actions are lower (with passing «goals» 0,5 meters wide).

In fact it did not happen.

Players strove to pass the wider «goal» with a higher speed, but increase in speed of movement resulted in that for players, who have been training dribbling only through the narrow «goal» (0,25 meters wide), hence with a lower speed, it became harder to handle the ball in these cases.

If players have been training the dribbling at a maximum speed with change of the direction of movement with certain requirements to the movements precision, while it was necessary to perform such dribbling with another requirements, there is no transition in speed and precision.

Fitness transition while using drills of various functional focus

The transition of precision (quickness and precision) of actions with the ball was considered for cases when the same skills (shots on goal, passes and dribbling) were trained on the background of loads of various functional focus.

During the experiment players have been performing following tasks.

Loads performed by players of different groups during the experimental trainings, on which background actions with the ball were trained		
In the 1st group: moving at a footpace and a run with small and medium power (aerobic load)	In the 2nd group: various actions (with and without the ball) with a high power during 10-20 seconds, repeating it at intervals, deficient for full recovery (aerobic-anaerobic load)	In the 3rd group: movements at 40-50 meters with an ultimate output, repeating it at intervals, enough for recovery (anaerobic load)

Results of experimental trainings have revealed the following:

– players, who have been training skills on the background of loads of small and medium power of actions (of aerobic nature), have slightly improved the quality of these skills performance in conditions of exactly low and medium power of actions;

– players, who have been training skills on the background of loads of maximum power of actions (of anaerobic nature), have slightly improve the quality of these skills performance in conditions of exactly maximum power, while certain players from this group have slightly improve the results in conditions of high power of actions;

– players, who have been training skills on the background of loads of high power of actions (of aerobic-anaerobic nature), have improved the quality of these skills performance in conditions of exactly high power, began to handle the ball in conditions of low and medium power of actions a bit more precisely, while certain players from this group have even begin to act with the ball slightly better in conditions of maximum power of actions (table 12).

Improvements in quality of actions with the ball of players, who have been training techniques on the background of loads of high power of actions, while performing these actions with the ball in test tasks on the background of loads of low and medium or maximum power is explained by the fact that aerobic-anaerobic loads include actions with maximum and low and medium power either.

For this reason there also was an insignificant improvement in quality of actions with the ball for certain players, who have been training techniques on the background of loads of maximum power of actions, when they performed these techniques on the background of high power of actions in test tasks.

Table 12. Comparison of results demonstrated by players, who have been training actions with the ball on the background of loads of various functional focus, while performing the same tasks before and after the experiment

Loads on which background actions with the ball were performed in test tasks		
load of low and medium power of actions (of aerobic nature)	load of high power of actions (of aerobic-anaerobic nature)	load of maximal power of actions (of anaerobic nature)
In the 1st group: **insignificant improvement in results**	In the 1st group: no change in results	In the 1st group: no change in results
In the 2nd group: **insignificant improvement in results**	In the 2nd group: **improvement in results**	In the 2nd group: **insignificant improvement in results of certain players**
In the 3rd group: no change in results	In the 3rd group: **insignificant improvement in results of certain players**	In the 3rd group: **improvement in results**

It is reputed that if players have been training techniques on the background of loads, providing one operational mode of work (one power of actions), while it is necessary to perform these techniques on the background of loads of another operational mode (with another power), there is virtually no transition of precision (speed and precision).

Precision transition while using drills having a local impact on leg muscles

The transition of precision (quickness and precision) of techniques performance was considered for cases when shots on goal, passes with a mounted trajectory and dribbling were trained with different condition of leg muscles (in the context of depletion of energy sources and concentration of cleavage products in these muscles) by the moment of performing of actions with the ball.

During the experiment players have been performing following tasks.

Loads performed by players of different groups during the experimental trainings directly before actions with the ball		
In the 1st group: without preliminary local load for leg muscles	In the 2nd group: local load for thigh flexor, resulting in depletion of phosphate energy sources in these muscles and concentration of cleavage products	In the 3rd group: local load for thigh extensor, resulting in depletion of phosphate energy sources in these muscles and concentration of cleavage products

Results of experimental trainings have revealed the following:
– players, who have been training actions with the ball without preliminary local load for leg muscles, have improved the quality of techniques performance exactly without preliminary local load for leg muscles;
– players, who have been training actions with the ball directly after a load upon thigh flexors, have improved the quality of techniques performance exactly after preliminary load upon thigh flexors;

– players, who have been training actions with the ball directly after a load upon thigh extensors, have improved the quality of techniques performance exactly after preliminary load upon thigh extensors (table 13).

Table 13. Comparison of results demonstrated by players, who have been training actions with the ball with different condition of leg muscles by the moment of the techniques performance, while performing the same tasks before and after the experiment

	Loads performed directly before actions with the ball in test tasks	
without a load on leg muscles	**local load on thigh flexors**	**local load on thigh extensors**
In the 1st group: **improvement in results**	In the 1st group: the same deterioration in results as before the experiment	In the 1st group: the same deterioration in results as before the experiment
In the 2nd group: insignificant deterioration in results	In the 2nd group: **improvement in results**	In the 2nd group: the same deterioration in results as before the experiment
In the 3rd group: insignificant deterioration in results	In the 3rd group: the same deterioration in results as before the experiment	In the 3rd group: **improvement in results**

If players have been training actions with the ball with certain condition of leg muscles (with certain level depletion of energy sources and concentration of cleavage products in these muscles), while it is necessary to perform these actions with another condition of leg muscles, there is no transition in precision (speed and precision).

Precision transition while using drills making various demands on displaying of motor sensitivity

The transition of precision of passes with a mounted trajectory and speed and precision of movements with the ball with change of direction of movement was considered for cases, when requirements to display of efforts differentiation while handling the ball were changing.

During the experiment tasks, which were based on methods of «simple repeats» and «contrasting tasks», were suggested to players (see Chapter 5 «Fundamentals, principles and methods of training the speed and precision of actions with the ball»).

Within the constraints the experiment players have been performing following tasks.

Tasks performed by players from different groups during the experimental trainings			
In the 1st group: maximally fast and precise movement with change of direction of movement with the ball of a standard weight	In the 2nd group: maximally fast and precise movement with change of direction of movement with the lightweight ball	In the 3rd group: maximally fast and precise movement with change of direction of movement with the weighted ball	In the 4th group: maximally fast and precise movements with change of direction of movement, alternating standard and lightweight balls from attempt to attempt («contrast tasks» method)

During the second experiment players have been performing following tasks.

Tasks performed by players from different groups during the experimental trainings	
In the 1st group: passes at an average distance with a mounted trajectory in space marked on the pitch surface each time («simple repeats» method)	In the 2nd group: passes at short and long distances with a mounted trajectory in space marked on the pitch surface alternately («contrast tasks» method)

Results of experimental trainings have revealed the following:
– in all cases players have improved results, performing movements with the ball in conditions they trained in;
– players, who have been training with the lightweight ball, have insignificantly improve results, performing movements with the ball of a standard weight;
– players, who have been alternating standard and lightweight balls in training, have significantly improved results, performing movements with the ball of a standard weight, and also began to handle the lightweight ball better;
– players, who have been training with the weighted ball, have worsened results, performing movements with standard and lightweight balls (table 14).

Results of experimental trainings have revealed the following:
– players, who have been training passes at an average distance with a mounted trajectory, have improved the precision of passes exactly at an average distance with a mounted trajectory;
– players, who have been training passes at short and long distances with a mounted trajectory, have improved the precision of passes, performed exactly at short and long distances with a mounted trajectory, and also the precision of

passes, performed at an average distance with a mounted trajectory (table 15).

Table 14. Comparison of results demonstrated by players, who have been training movements with the ball of different weight, while performing the same tasks before and after the experiment

Test tasks			
movement with the ball of a standard weight	movement with lightweight ball	movement with weighted ball	movement with alternating of standard and lightweight balls from attempt to attempt
In the 1st group: **improvement in results**	In the 1st group: no change in results	In the 1st group: no change in results	In the 1st group: **insignificant improvement in results**
In the 2nd group: **insignificant improvement in results**	In the 2nd group: **improvement in results**	In the 2nd group: no change in results	In the 2nd group: **insignificant improvement in results**
In the 3rd group: deterioration in results	In the 3rd group: deterioration in results	In the 3rd group: **improvement in results**	In the 3rd group: deterioration in results
In the 4th group: **significant improvement in results**	In the 4th group: **improvement in results**	In the 4th group: no change in results	In the 4th group: **significant improvement in results**

Table 15. Comparison of results demonstrated by players, who have been training actions with the ball with methods of «simple repeats» and «contrast tasks», while performing the same tasks before and after the experiment

Test tasks	
passes with a mounted trajectory into space marked on the pitch surface each time at an average distance («simple repeats» method)	passes with a mounted trajectory into spaces marked on the pitch surface at short and long distances alternately («contrast tasks» method)
In the 1st group: improvement in results	In the 1st group: no change in results
In the 2nd group: improvement in results	In the 2nd group: improvement in results

If players were training actions with the ball in more complicated conditions (in the context of requirements for displaying of motor sensitivity), while it is necessary to perform these actions in more simple conditions (in the context of requirements for displaying of motor sensitivity), there is a transition of precision (quickness and precision).

Precision transition while using drills making various demands on visual perception

The transition of precision of shots on target with a foot while using drills, in which there are different requirements for visual perception, was considered for cases, when players could track the ball in a different time before the shot, and also for cases, when players have been kicking the ball sent to them with different trajectories.

During the first experiment players have been performing following tasks.

Tasks performed by players from different groups during the experimental trainings	
In the 1st group: shots on target with a foot on a rolling ball with a first touch, tracking its movement for a short time	**In the 2nd group:** shots on target with a foot on a rolling ball with a first touch, tracking its movement long enough

During the second experiment players have been performing following tasks.

Tasks performed by players from different groups during the experimental trainings	
In the 1st group: shots on target with a foot on a rolling ball with a first touch, when the ball approached to the player along a straight path after coming in his sight	**In the 2nd group:** shots on target with a foot on a moving ball with a first touch, when the ball approached to the player after coming in his sight, changing trajectory of movement after rebound off the reflecting panel

Results of experimental trainings have revealed the following:

– players, who have been training shots on target with a foot on a rolling ball with a first touch, tracking its movement long enough, have improved the precision of shots, performed exactly with relatively long time of tracking the ball;

– players, who have been training shots on target with a foot on a rolling ball with a first touch, tracking its movement for a short time, have improved the precision of shots performed with a short time of tracking, and also began to perform shots much more precisely, while tracking the ball's movements for sufficiently long time (table 16).

Table 16. Comparison of results demonstrated by players, who have been training shots on goal with a foot on a rolling ball with different time of its tracking, while performing the same test tasks before and after the experiment

Test tasks	
shots on target with a foot on a rolling ball with a first touch, tracking its movement for a short time	shots on target with a foot on a rolling ball with a first touch, tracking its movement long enough
In the 1st group: **improvement in results**	In the 1st group: **significant improvement in results**
In the 2nd group: no change in results	In the 2nd group: **improvement in results**

Results of experimental trainings have revealed the following:

– players, who have been training shots on target with a foot and with a first touch, when the ball approached to them along a straight path, have improved the precision of shots, performed exactly when the ball approached to them along a straight path;

– players, who have been training shots on target with a first touch, when the ball approached to them after rebound off the reflecting panel, have improved the precision of shots, performed either when the ball approached to them after rebound off the reflecting panel and along a straight path (table 17).

Experiments conducted with goalkeepers in football and hockey, and in such sports as volleyball and tennis, have also revealed that if players train to block the ball in more difficult condition in the context of visual perception, they improve results not only in these conditions, but also in simpler conditions in the context of requirements for visual perception, even if they didn't train in these simple conditions.

Table 17. Comparison of results demonstrated by players, who have been training shots with a foot on a rolling ball with different trajectories of its movement, while performing the same test tasks before and after the experiment

Test tasks	
shots on target with a foot on a rolling ball with a first touch, when the ball approached to the player after coming in his sight along a straight path	shots on target with a foot on a rolling ball with a first touch, when the ball approached to the player after coming in his sight, bouncing off the reflecting panel
In the 1st group: improvement in results	In the 1st group: no change in results
In the 2nd group: improvement in results	In the 2nd group: improvement in results

If players were training actions with the ball in more complicated conditions (in the context of requirements for oculogyric reactions), while it is necessary to perform these actions in more simple conditions (in the context of requirements for oculogyric reactions), there is a transition of precision (quickness and precision).

Impact of anaerobic and glycolytic drills on speed and precision of players' actions

The transition of speed and precision of actions with the ball while using anaerobic and glycolytic drills, aimed at development of so called speed endurance, was considered for cases when these drills were or weren't performed before training movements with the ball with following pass with a mounted trajectory.

During the experiment players have been performing following tasks.

Tasks performed by players from different groups during the experimental trainings	
In the 1st group: maximally fast and precise movement with the ball with change of direction of movement and following quick pass with a mounted trajectory into space marked on the pitch surface	**In the 2nd group:** the load of anaerobic and glycolytic nature 1 minute long was performed directly before maximally fast and precise movement with the ball with change of direction of movement and following quick pass with a mounted trajectory into space marked on the pitch surface

Results of experimental trainings have revealed the following:

– players, who have been training quick and precise movement with the ball with following quick pass with a mounted trajectory without a preliminary load of anaerobic and glycolytic nature, have slightly improved results, when it was necessary to perform these actions exactly without such preliminary load;

– players, who have been training quick and precise movement with the ball with following quick pass with a mounted trajectory after performing a preliminary load of anaerobic and glycolytic nature, have decreased results, when it was necessary to perform these actions exactly without such preliminary load in test tasks (table 18).

Reduction of results of players, who have been training actions with the ball directly after a load of anaerobic and glycolytic nature, in cases when it was necessary to perform these actions without such load, may be explained with the following.

Drills of anaerobic and glycolytic nature, in which players have to act with a high lactate concentration in peripheral blood for a long time, force players to act with the ball right after at a lower speed comparing to those they could have acted at in case there is no such preliminary load.

Table 18. Comparison of results demonstrated by players, who have been training actions with the ball after a load of anaerobic and glycolytic nature and without it, while performing the same test tasks before and after the experiment

Loads performed directly before movement with the ball and following pass with a mounted trajectory in test tasks	
without a load	load of anaerobic and glycolytic nature 1 minute long
In the 1st group: **improvement in results**	In the 1st group: the same deterioration in results as before the experiment
In the 2nd group: deterioration in results	In the 2nd group: **improvement in results**

For this reason players, who have been training dribbling and passes directly after a load of anaerobic and glycolytic nature during the experiment, have virtually been training these techniques acting not with a maximum speed, and have obviously consolidated the structure of movements with the ball, performed without maximum speed.

When after the end of the experiment these player have been performing these techniques without a preliminary load of anaerobic and glycolytic nature, they spontaneously kept the structure of movements developed earlier, and consequently decreased results they had demonstrated before the beginning of the experiment while performing actions with the ball without a preliminary load of anaerobic and glycolytic nature, although there were no immediate causes for reduction of results.

Directly after performing drills of anaerobic and glycolytic nature players don't act with the ball with a maximum speed (individual for everyone). Permanent use of such drills during the relatively long period of time results in that players begin to act with the ball not with a maximum possible speed even in cases, when there is no preliminary load of anaerobic and glycolytic nature.

Resume

Conditions, in which players train actions with the ball, and conditions, in which they have to perform these actions in competitive games, may differ by the following features:
– the quickness of techniques performance; value of efforts applied by players to perform actions with the ball; the external shape of movements with the ball (on kinematic and dynamic characteristics);
– players' fitness shape in whole and condition of leg muscles by the moment of performing of actions with the ball;
– requirements for visual perception and displaying of motor sensitivity.

In cases when players have been training actions with the ball in certain conditions, while it is necessary to perform in conditions, in which these actions weren't trained earlier, the transition of fitness in precision (speed and precision) of techniques performance may either happen or not.

Conditions in which players have been training actions with the ball	Performing of actions with the ball in conditions differ from conditions of previous trainings
With a certain kinematics, dynamics and coordination of muscle work	There is **no transition** of precision (speed and precision)
On the background of loads of various functional focus	There is **no transition** of precision (speed and precision)
After preliminary local load for leg muscles	There is **no transition** of precision (speed and precision)
With certain requirements for visual perception and displaying of motor sensitivity	One-way **transition** of fitness from more difficult conditions to easier in the context of requirements for sensory systems work
After preliminary load of anaerobic and glycolytic nature	**Negative transition of speed and precision**

For notes

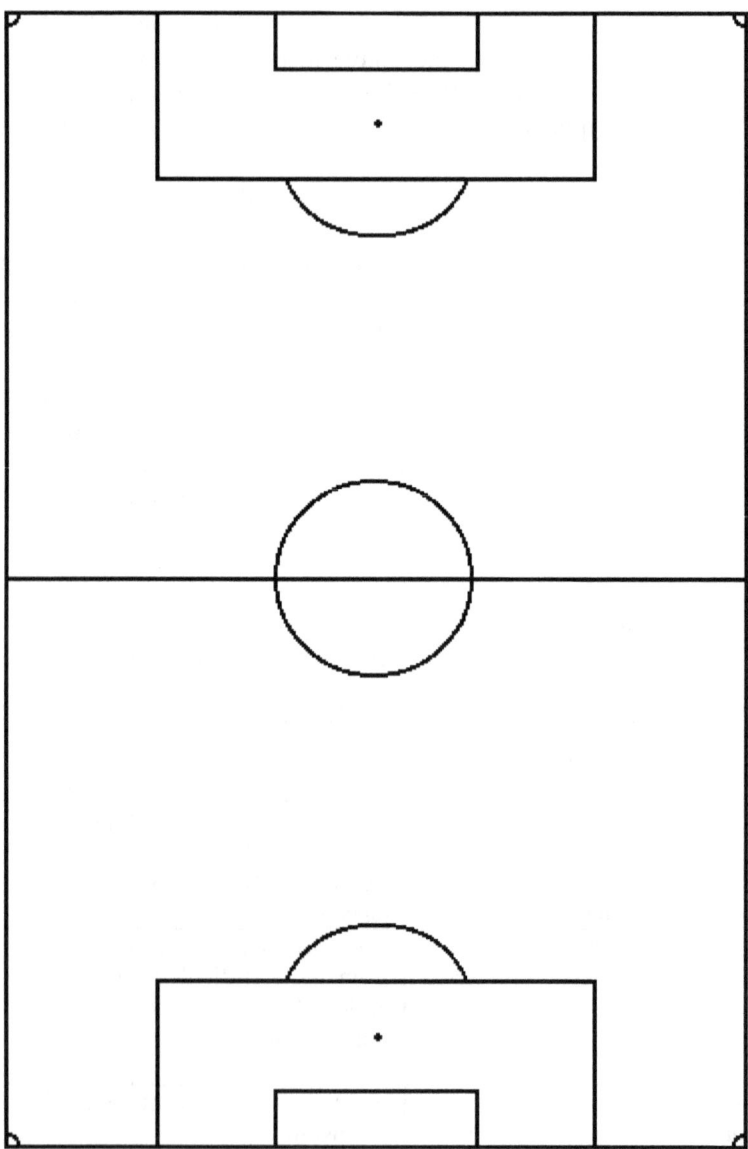

CHAPTER 5. FUNDAMENTALS, PRINCIPLES AND METHODS OF TRAINING THE SPEED AND PRECISION OF ACTIONS WITH THE BALL

Introduction

Unlike the term of «technical preparation» the phrase «precision training» is unusual a bit, though it is unlikely that someone would dispute the fact that skilled players, while training the techniques, virtually try to achieve the increasing in speed and precision of its performance.

Fundamentals, principles and most significant methods of training the speed and precision of actions with the ball by players. They are developed on the ground of the results of researches in football and other sport games, conducted to explore:

– individual characteristics of display of precision in movement;
– building of fast and precise sport movements with the ball;
– impact of various factors on speed and precision of players' actions with the ball;
– transition of fitness in speed and precision of techniques performance by players.

Components of players' special working efficiency

In football there may be just a job done, but also a useful work may be made. The efficiency criteria of a work performed in competitive matches always was and will be the precision of techniques performance.

There is a little use of players who consistently make mistakes while interacting with the ball, even if they're able to run a lot.

Players' special working efficiency consists in combination of a high motor activity and precise (fast and precise) work with the ball.

Football working efficiency consists not only of how a player may play in competitive matches, but also how he can transit training loads (repeatedly repeat certain skills in exercise, perform a large amount of actions with the ball within training, withstand trainings in general). For example, there are players, who may brilliantly play in one or two matches, though don't fit in team, because cannot withstand heavy training loads.

The ability to combine the high motor activity and the precision of actions with the ball is the a hallmark of skilled players. Researches have revealed, that when players of different qualification perform actions with the ball on the background of the same working load, players of a higher class are able to repeat techniques a higher number of times, and with a high precision all the time.

The amount of a special work with the ball with the necessary precision, that may be performed by player in game and training, is determined by three main factors:

– the level of grasping the structure of motor actions with the ball;

– the level of development of motor characteristics and functional capabilities;

– the condition of sensory systems (fig. 24).

A high level of players' special working efficiency suggests the harmonious blend of all its components, as a lag in one of components or a slant on course of training towards the another result in reduce of performance level.

Correspondingly the work on perfection of the technique of possession, increasing of motor characteristics and functional capabilities and development of sensory systems should performed in parallel, in which connection certain principles, based on laws of fitness transition, should be complied during the training of each of these components.

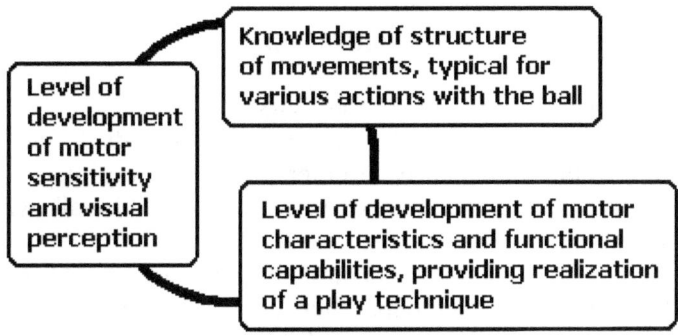

Fig. 24. Basic components of players' special working efficiency

Perfection of actions with the ball

If players would train not the technique they would need in competitive games, they'd have to use the technique they've been training in these games.

It is impossible to train the technical performance of actions with the ball, that would be necessary in competitive games, without observing the principle of specialization.

The specialization means the degree of coincidence of training tasks with one or other episodes of competitive games on:

– coordination of player's muscle work («inner» organization of movements);

– kinematic and dynamic characteristics (quickness of players' movements; value of efforts applied by players to perform actions with the ball; quickness of performance and the external shape of movements with the ball);

– players' fitness shape in whole and condition of their leg muscles.

There is no limit for perfection of the precision of players' actions with the ball, and great skill may be achieved either by those who are gifted by nature to a greater extent and those who are less talented.

Terms of observance of principle of specialization

Coordination of muscle activity

If on course of performance of training drills players' muscles would «talk» to each other not in the way they do in competitive games, then in such games they would «talk with a training accent».

It is impossible to control the interaction of certain muscles and muscle groups, but we could suspect, which intermuscular coordination would be trained, on what tasks would be performed in a training drill and in what conditions players are destined to act with the ball.

The reason for such suggestion is that the range of mistakes, allowable for players in certain situation, decreases or increases with change in requirements for techniques performance, and the coordination of muscle work changes correspondingly.

It is necessary to set the same demands for techniques performance by players that apply in competitive games, for players to really improve play actions with the ball.

For example, there is no reason for skilled players to train shots on goal on a stationary ball in conditions when there is no countering and no need for quickness of a shot performance, and also there is no wall from defending players, because shots on goal aren't performed in such conditions in games.

Kinematics and dynamics of motor actions

Concepts of «difficult» and «easy» in technique of possession may be considered in the context of learning techniques and performing techniques already learned. There is no doubt that it is much harder to learn, for example, an overhead (scissor) kick, than a kick on the stationary ball, though concepts of «difficult» and «easy» change their meaning when we're talking about performing techniques learned earlier.

The precision of skilled players' actions with the ball, regardless of whether these actions «difficult» or «easy», is determined only with how familiar for players they are.

Players who train dribbling with change of direction of movement only at low speed would not begin to act with the ball better, moving at a maximum speed. Players who train dribbling with change of direction of movement only at a high speed all the time would improve skill in handling the ball exactly a this speed, but the ability to handle the ball while moving with change of direction at a low speed would remain the same.

Exercising shots on goal with an ultimate output and sending the ball with a linear trajectory would not allow to improve the precision of shots with sending the ball at a high mounted trajectory. However much players would train shots on goal with sending the ball positioned on the pitch surface, it would not help them to improve the precision of kicks on the ball positioned at some height above the pitch surface, neither in supporting position, nor while diving moreover.

Essentially training can make any play actions with the ball well-known and familiar for players, but for this it is necessary for players, while repeating a certain technique, to act exactly with the quickness, move exactly with the speed, display exactly those efforts, which are required for this technique to be performed with in competitive games.

Conditions of drills, in which actions with the ball are improved, should be no less, but also no more difficult, than conditions of one or other episodes of competitive games. In this context shots on goal in 18-yard box at an angle to the goal obligingly with physical contact with the opponent should be also performed in training to improve the precision of such shots.

Specialization of a physiological load

To be in familiar conditions means, above all, to be in familiar conditions in the context of various organs and systems functioning. Therefore it is necessary for players to work in training in modes they have to act in during competitive games to improve play actions with the ball.

In competitive games actions with the ball are performed in three quite clearly distinguished zones of power emergence (low and medium, high, maximal), and so players have to train techniques with demonstration of relevant power of actions.

It is very important that immediate performers of actions – muscles – are in condition they are during competitive games, as overloaded or, vice versa, too «fresh» muscles (comparing to their condition in competitive games) would not work in the way it is necessary.

A drill may be constructed so that players would be in a fitness shape, corresponding to one or another episode of the competitive game, while performing it, but at the same time the condition of certain muscles would be far from that in the competitive game because of additional impact on them (local load). A game when there are additional poundage on players (weighted belts or blades) may set the example of such drill.

The principle of specialization of physiological load is a reflection of a fact that while training actions with the ball on course of drills players have to be in a fitness shape which corresponds to a certain game episode in each repeat, with any non-specialized loads of local nature on leg muscles should be excluded.

Performing a large amount of techniques repeats in specialized conditions as one of the most important conditions of training of speed and precision of actions with the ball

If players act with the ball (even very much) in non-specialized conditions, they don't improve abilities necessary in competitive games.

Important are not the volumes of techniques performance in themselves, but the volumes of techniques repeats exactly in specialized conditions in the context of players' fitness shape and technique of performance of actions with the ball.

Competitive game could become the best specialized training drill, but players contact with the ball during matches not so often.

Therefore there is virtually one way for players to gain a large amount of techniques repeats in specialized conditions - to train actions with the ball simulating those which are performed in one or another episode of competitive games, repeating them multiply.

Frequency of these actions repetitions is limited with «physiological barriers». If relevant regulations of drills performance, allowing players to work with a necessary power of actions, are not observed, than larger amounts of techniques repetitions may be gained, but performed technically not like in competitive games.

Development of motor characteristics

Display of motor characteristics is anyway related with how players act with the ball at the last.

It makes no sense for players to train strength, quickness and stamina just to be strong, fast and endurant. These qualities should provide the precision of players' actions with the ball during each game and each training, run of sessions and all the competitive period.

Therefore the main principles, which are important to observe while developing skilled players' motor characteristics, are:

– reaching necessary and sufficient levels;
– coherence of work on motor characteristics and technique of possession.

Reaching the necessary and sufficient levels

The importance of development of motor characteristics is obvious: players won't be able to act with the ball at a high speed in case they cannot run fast, and won't be able to shoot with a head in high jump if the cannot jump high.

It is inappropriate though to pay the development of motor characteristics more attention, than is necessary for proficient performance of actions with the ball in competitive games.

It also has to be noted that different forms of motor characteristics display take training impact to different extents, and so, when skilled players try to develop the motor characteristic that is eminently conservative, they just support the opportunities of its display at a level reached earlier.

Coherence of work on motor characteristics and technique of possession

It is known that during puberty, when the natural development of locomotor system breaks loose, children movements are atactic and not particularly accurate. At this time the dynamic compliance that was between motor characteristics and motor programs of various actions, developed earlier, breaks.

When skilled players develop motor characteristics intentionally and during the long period of time, completely forgetting about the ball, the compliance between the technique of possession and motor characteristics may also break, which results in increasing of mistakes while performing actions with the ball.

At the same time, if players who have significantly decreased their physical conditions for various reasons, get in conditions where they have to display maximum quickness and efforts, not only the reduction in the quality of actions with the ball, but also the risk of getting injured occurs.

Players, either young or mature, may perform techniques with a maximum precision, if the level of their motor characteristics corresponds with current motor programs of actions with the ball.

At any stage of players' long-term training motor characteristics should provide the realization of motor programs of actions with the ball in different conditions.

This is possible providing that the training of the precision of techniques performance would go in **parallel** to their development.

The principle of parallelism in this case provides two variants of work depending on what training resources (drills) would be applied for development of motor characteristics:

– if specific, when tasks of development of motor characteristics and improving the technique of possession may be performed simultaneously in one drill (adjoint method) with the essential condition that the principle of specialization is not broken in the context of players' fitness shape and performing motor actions with the ball (coordination of muscle work; kinematic and dynamic characteristics: players' speed of movement, value of efforts applied by players to perform actions with the ball, quickness of performance and the external shape of movements with the ball);

– if non-specific, then these tasks should be decided in different drills at one training (drills for perfection of technique of actions with the ball are performed first, and then drills to develop motor characteristics) or at trainings following one after another to avoid the impact of so-called «first effect» of using non-specific tasks.

Developing modes in drills with the ball

Development of motor characteristics provides the use of certain so-called developing modes of work.

What may happen, if players would improve the technique of actions with the ball in these modes?

When in drills with the balls there are one or another conditions (certain intensity of drills, duration of pauses between work and rest), players perform actions with the ball with efforts and power, which are suggested by given conditions.

In these cases there will be some characteristics in technique of skills performance, specific exactly for modes of work in which players have to act.

If working modes in drills with the ball don't coincide with modes that occur in competitive games (when physiological changes in the players' body on course of the drill are not comparable to changes occurring in one or another game episode), players would virtually train actions with the ball differ from those performed in competitive games.

For example, what happens, when in training there are large amounts of drills with the ball, which regulation provides the development of anaerobic and glycolytic mechanism of energy supply (speed endurance)?

The development of this mechanism is going in conditions which virtually aren't observed in games. Therefore, with consistent performance of drills with the ball of anaerobic and glycolytic nature for a long time, there occurs undesired changes in speed and precision of players' actions with the ball in competitive matches (see Chapter 4 «Transition of fitness in speed and precision of actions with the ball»).

It is reasonable to develop motor characteristics in drills with the ball, when given modes of work necessary for development of these characteristics coincide with players' working modes in competitive games.

In other cases issues of motor characteristics development and perfection of technique of possession should be decided in different drills.

First effect of non-specific load impact

Football is a powerful physical drill that has a significant impact on the players' body, but this impact is not always sufficient to develop motor characteristics to the extent it is required in football of a high level.

Repetition of only one or another play episodes in training also doesn't allow players to develop all motor characteristics, necessary for performing on competitive games.

Therefore players have to use various drills from other sports (field-and-track, weightlifting, gymnastic) to increase the level of strength, quickness, stamina and flexibility. After such drills it is necessary to adapt technique to changes occurred in the body, though it has to be noted that non-specific drills affect the quality of actions with the ball, performed directly after, negatively (see Chapter 3 «Impact of various factors on the precision of actions with the ball»).

Firstly it refers to drills having heavy influence (uncharacteristic for football) on leg muscles, which become into new unfamiliar overwrought condition after such impact.

In this regard it is necessary to switch to work with the ball after non-specific drills after a while, when first effect of these drills impact is gone.

This time may be from several seconds to several hours depending on impact of non-specific load, as muscles would need one time to recover after performing a set of jumps over obstacles, and quite another – after squatting with heavy poundage.

It is not only ineffectively, but in many cases quite destructively to train actions with the ball, which have heavy influence, directly after performing non-specific drills. For example, there is a risk of injuries right after strength exercises with heavy weights, except that leg muscles are not prepared to work with the ball, if a player would perform powerful speed-ups and jumps, running at a maximum speed.

If non-specific drills, which have an uncharacteristic for football impact on players, are applied for development of motor characteristics, then it is necessary to begin working with the ball after some time (more or less depending on impact of non-specific load) to avoid the negative impact of a first effect of using such drills.

Development of sensory systems

There is no point to overestimate the meaning of sensory systems for precise techniques performance, though it is obvious that without necessary level of their development the quality operating with the ball is hindered. That's why it is preferable to pay some attention to development of motor sensitivity and visual perception.

For skilled players it is enough to maintain motor sensitivity and visual perception in necessary «shape», making them operational before games and trainings.

There is no particular need to provide special time for development of motor sensitivity and certainly visual perception by skilled outfield players, excluding cases when it is necessary to restore «the ball fell», lost during the holiday or medical treatment, or when the learning of new techniques begins.

The main principle of development of sensory systems is the setting of a task harder than the central one

Fitness transition while developing sensory systems is going only in one direction: from more difficult conditions to easier in the context of requirements for visual perception and display of motor sensitivity.

Therefore the one principle form the basis of all sensory systems: **setting the task harder than the basic one in the context of requirements for visual perception and display of motor sensitivity.**

What conditions may be considered to be the most difficult for sensory systems work?

The most difficult for players in the context of visual perception are:

– tracking the ball flying with complex unpredictable trajectories;

– receiving and reflecting the flying ball with small time of its tracking and with a lower illumination.

Therefore the basic method for improving visual perception **is performing tasks at the breaking point of perception of the ball.** We should underline that the issue is the saturation point of visual perception exactly and not players' physical abilities.

In the context of visual sensitivity it is harder for players while performing techniques to:
– differentiate small efforts and low speed of own movements;
– alternately perform actions, differing markedly on value of efforts, speed and amplitude of movements performance;
– act with a lightweight ball or a smaller ball (comparing to a standard ball).

Methods of development of motor sensitivity

Methods of training of motor sensitivity – performing contrast and pulled together tasks – were developed on the basis of the principle of development of sensory systems «setting the task harder than the basic one».

The defining attribute of drills constructed on the basis of methods of contrast and pulled together tasks is that the change of efforts while touching the ball or the change of direction of sending the ball either height-wise or in a horizontal plane should occur during their performance.

Requirements for the precision of actions with the ball in the same drill or in drills following one after another also could change.

Motor sensitivity may be fully realized in a range (in movement amplitude), in which its development was going. Since it is necessary for players to have exactly «the football ball feel», there is no sense to go beyond football drills while developing or maintaining their motor sensitivity.

Contrast tasks method

Contrast tasks method provides performance of actions with the ball, differing markedly in efforts displayed by a player, for example the alternation of shots on goal with sending the ball on a high mounted and close to linear trajectories, passes at a short and long distances, varying the speed of movement with the ball.

Basic action with the ball «interrupted» with a contrast one, with the biggest effect is observed in case when contrast actions make up a quarter of total volume of this technique repetitions.

One of the most effective variants of contrast tasks is the performance of actions alternately with the standard and lightweight ball (varying of the ball weight). On the background of motor sensitivity, heightened by means of handling the lightweight ball, players may achieve the higher precision of actions with the standard ball. Due to the fact that actions with the lightweight ball differ from the play ones, their share should not exceed 25 per cent of time of the whole task or total amount of performed actions with the ball).

It is necessary to finish the task with the standard ball, so players would have necessary muscular sensations in their memory.

Pulled together tasks method

Basis for the method of pulled together tasks was provided with a phenomenon discovered by Russian physiologist I. Pavlov, which he called «differentiating inhibition». The essence of this method is as follows.

The same action with the ball is repeated consequently many times, with first attempts should differ markedly on characteristics of sending the ball (on distance, on direction) or quickness of performance.

Following repetitions are performed in a way that the difference in characteristics of sending the ball or quickness of performance of action with the ball becomes smaller and smaller.

Resume

On the basis of researches following basic fundamentals, principles and methods of training the speed and precision of actions with the ball by players.

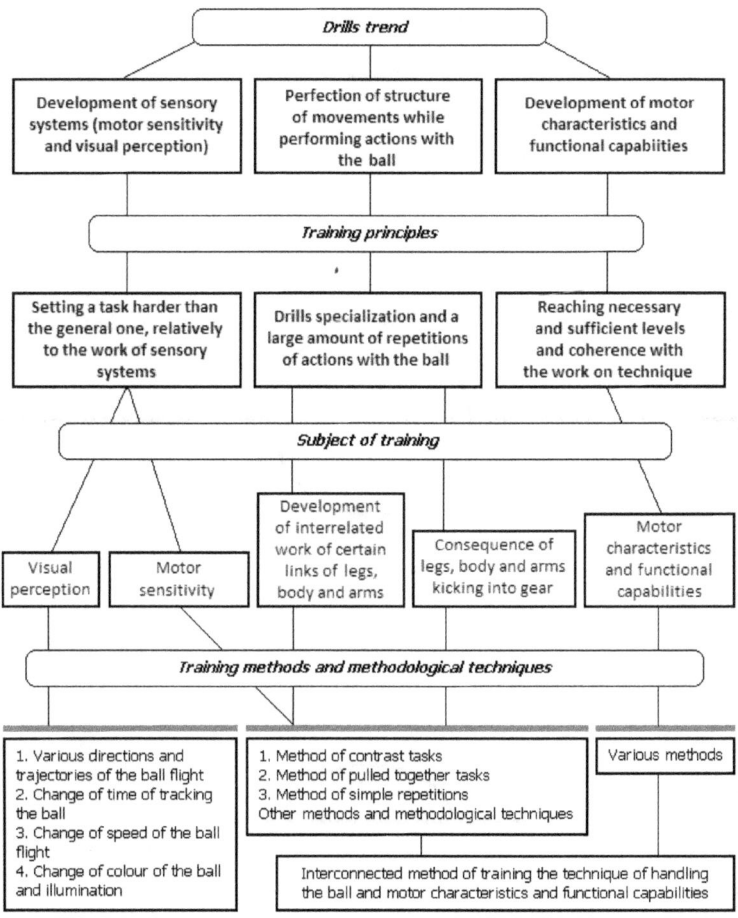

For notes

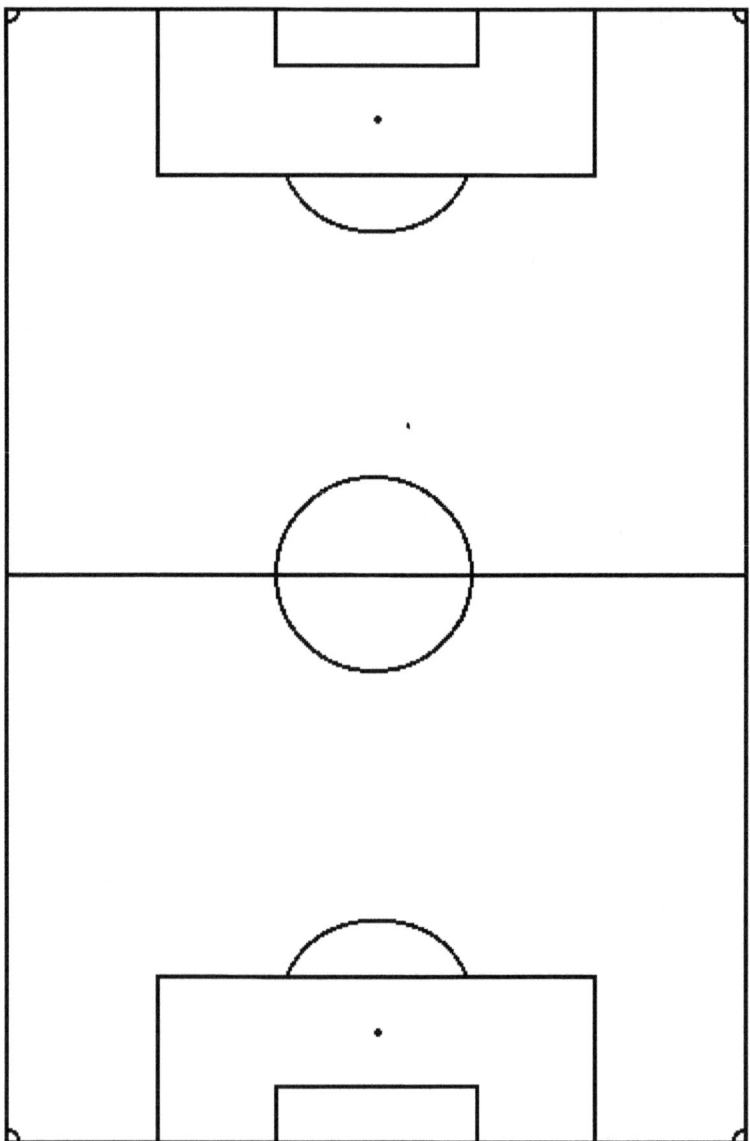

AFTERWORD

First. The criteria of the efficiency of possession technique in football may be the precision (speed and precision in combination) of players' actions with the ball.

Second. The level of the technical prowess of skilled players is determined:

– by 50-70 per cent – inherited ability to perform any movements precisely;

– by 20-45 per cent – abilities to perform certain actions with the ball, developed in training (level of fitness), developed in trainings;

– by 5-10 per cent – the level of development of motor sensitivity («the ball feel»).

Third. If it is necessary to show certain strength, quickness, stamina to perform single action with the ball or some exercise, insufficient level of these characteristics may become a limiting factor for precise performances of techniques.

Fourth. In the context of biomechanics the quality of actions with the ball depends on how well motor programs of these actions are developed, which represent the kicking of various body parts into gear in different situations in such sequence that the conclusive phase of a strike motion lasts for defined time.

Fifth. Development of motor programs of actions with the ball begins from the first kick on the ball, which may be performed at the earliest age. Motor interactions between certain body parts, peculiar mostly to more simple actions, develop first, and then – to actions with the ball of any complexity.

With looping of actions with the ball with determination to their quick and precise performance players gradually achieve that the duration of realization phase of a strike motion becomes more constant on time, while the time of pre-realization phase decreases. This allows them to act with the ball more precisely and quicker that earlier.

Sixth. Various external factors may affect the quality of players' actions with the ball positively or negatively. The extent and nature of change of speed and precision of techniques performance under certain impact are determined by the presence of the practical experience of meetings with this impact.

Seventh. The efficiency of drills, suggested to skilled players for perfecting the play technique, is determined by whether fitness transition from training conditions to competitive occurs with their use (whether an accumulative effect in the precision of actions with the ball is achieved after applying these drills for a relatively long time).

Eighth. Conditions, in which players train actions with the ball, may differ from conditions of competitive games episodes on the following indicators:

– kinematic and dynamic characteristics of players' movements;

– players' fitness shape in whole and condition of leg muscles by the moment of performing of actions with the ball;

– requirements for visual perception and displaying of motor sensitivity.

If players have been training actions with the ball in certain conditions, while it is necessary to perform in conditions, in which these actions weren't trained earlier, the transition of speed and precision of techniques performance may either happen or not.

Ninth. Players' special working efficiency in trainings and games suggests a combination of a high motor activity and fast and precise handling with the ball.

Tenth. Work on perfection of basic components of players' special working efficiency (play technique, motor characteristics and functional capabilities, sensory systems) should be performed in parallel, observing certain principles, based on laws of fitness transition, while training each of them.

BIBLIOGRAPHY

Абдул Сахиб Аль Джамшир. Влияние физической нагрузки на точность двигательных действий футболистов: автореф. дис. ... канд. пед. наук / Абдул Сахиб Аль Джамшир; ГЦОЛИФК. – М., 1987. – 23 с.

Бабуджян С.Г. Исследование путей совершенствования точности ударных действий футболистов в специальных заданиях: автореф. дис. ... канд. пед. наук / С.Г. Бабуджян; ВНИИФК. – М., 1978. – 27 с.

Бакшин С.Г. Оценка пространственно-временных характеристик двигательной деятельности футболистов высокой квалификации: автореф. дис. ... канд. пед. наук / С.Г. Бакшин; МОГИФК. – Малаховка, 1987. – 22 с.

Безъязычный Б.И. Формирование ударных движений по показателям целевой точности у юных спортсменов 12-16 лет (на примере футбола): автореф. дис. ... канд. пед. наук / Б.И. Безъязычный; ГПИ им. Г.С. Сковороды. – Харьков, 1991. – 23 с.

Белов А.С. Сравнительная оценка факторов, определяющих точность движения спортсменов в специальных заданиях и экспериментальное обоснование их совершенствования: автореф. дисс. ... канд. пед. наук / А.С. Белов; ГЦОЛИФК. – М., 1972. – 18 с.

Бен Саид Нуреддин. Влияние физической нагрузки анаэробно-гликолитической направленности на точность двигательных действий футболистов: автореф. дис. ... канд. пед. наук / Бен Саид Нуреддин; РГАФК. – М., 1998. – 26 с.

Бен Саид Нуреддин, Голомазов С. Влияние специализированности нагрузки анаэробно-гликолитической направленности на точность двигательных действий футболистов / Бен Саид Нуреддин, С. Голомазов // Теория и практика футбола. – 1999. – № 1.

Блащак И.М. Точность ударов по воротам в соревнованиях и тренировках футболистов и факторы, ее определяющие: автореф. дис. ... канд. пед. наук / И.М. Блащак; ГЦОЛИФК. – М., 1991. – 22 с.

Бутаев В.К. Влияние нагрузки на технику движений, требующих целевой точности: автореф. дис. ... канд. пед. наук / В.К. Бутаев; ГЦОЛИФК. – М., 1990. – 21 с.

Вайнбаум Я.С. Управление движениями и совершенствование технической подготовки в физическом воспитании / Я.С. Вайнбаум. – М., 1981. – 38 с.

Верхошанский Ю.В. Основы специальной физической подготовки спортсменов / Ю.В. Верхошанский. – М.: Физкультура и спорт, 1988. – 332 с.

Вовк С.И. Динамика специализированных ощущений и восприятий при перерывах в тренировочном процессе у квалифицированных спортсменов / С.И. Вовк // VII Международный научный конгресс «Современный олимпийский спорт и спорт для всех». Материалы конференции. – Том 3. – М., РГУФК, 2003. – С. 152-153.

Волков Н.И., Ромашов А.В. Утомление при упражнениях умеренной мощности и координация функций / Н.И. Волков, А.В. Ромашов // «Физиологическая характеристика и методы определения выносливости в спорте». – М.: Физкультура и спорт, 1972. – С. 140-147.

Гагаева Г.М. Психология футбола / Г.М. Гагаева. – М.: Физкультура и спорт, 1968. – 214 с.

Голомазов С.В. Психологические особенности организации точностных движений в играх / С.В. Голомазов // Психолого-педагогические проблемы спортивных игр. Под ред. Родионова А.В. – М., ВНИИФК, 1989. – С. 50-53.

Голомазов С.В. Кинезиология точностных действий человека / С.В. Голомазов. – М.: СпортАкадемПресс, 2003. – 227 с.

Голомазов С.В., Зациорский В.М. Точность двигательных действий: учебное пособие / С.В. Голомазов, В.М. Зациорский. – М., 1979. – 26 с.

Голомазов С.В. и др. Состояние мышечного аппарата, как фактор, определяющий точность целенаправленного двигательного действия / С.В. Голомазов, М. Кадри, В.Н. Селуянов, М. Шейх // Теория и практика физической культуры. – 1994. – № 11. – С. 28-31.

Голомазов С., Зациорский В., Чирва Б. Меткость, точность и техника действий с мячом и принципиальные подходы к тренировке точности быстрых движений / С. Голомазов, В. Зациорский, Б. Чирва // Теория и практика футбола. – 2004. – № 1. – С. 33-35.

Голомазов С., Чирва Б. Футбол. Тренировка точности юных спортсменов / С. Голомазов, Б. Чирва. – М., РГАФК, 1994. – 81 с.

Голомазов С., Чирва Б. Футбол. Причины технического брака: метод. разработки для слушателей ВШТ. Выпуск 4 / С. Голомазов, Б. Чирва. – М., РГАФК, 1998. – 51 с.

Голомазов С., Чирва Б. Футбол. Быстрота и точность действий с мячом: метод. разработки для слушателей ВШТ. Выпуск 6 / С. Голомазов, Б. Чирва. – М., РГАФК, 1998. – 51 с.

Голомазов С., Чирва Б. Футбол. Основы и организация тренировки точности технических приемов: метод. разработки для слушателей ВШТ. Выпуск 7 / С. Голомазов, Б. Чирва. – М., РГАФК, 1998. – 51 с.

Голомазов С., Чирва Б. Футбол. Проблема адаптации техники: метод. пособие. Выпуск 15 / С. Голомазов, Б. Чирва. – М., РГАФК, 2000. – 31 с.

Голомазов С.В., Чирва Б.Г. Футбол. Теоретические основы совершенствования точности действий с мячом / С.В. Голомазов, Б.Г. Чирва – М.: ТВТ Дивизион, 2006. – 112 с.

Голомазов С.В., Чирва Б.Г. Теория и методика футбола. Том 1. Техника игры / С.В. Голомазов, Б.Г. Чирва. – М.: ТВТ Дивизион, 2008. – 475 с.

Губа В.П., Лексаков А.В. Теория и методика футбола: учебник / В.П. Губа, А.В. Лексаков. – М.: Советский спорт, 2013. – 536 с.

Гусейнов Ф.А. Влияние утомления на двигательную структуру бега на различные дистанции и пути совершенствования технического мастерства: автореф. дис. ... канд. пед. наук / Ф.А. Гусейнов; ГЦОЛИФК. – М., 1983. – 19 с.

Джамиль Салех Махди. Точность двигательных действий, выполняемых с максимальной быстротой, у футболистов: автореф. дис. ... канд. пед. наук / Джамиль Салех Махди; ГЦОЛИФК. – М., 1984. – 23 с.

Донской Д.Д. Биомеханика с основами спортивной техники / Д.Д. Донской. – М.: Физкультура и спорт, 1971. – 288 с.

Дьячков В.М. Совершенствование технического мастерства спортсменов / В.М. Дьячков. – М.: Физкультура и спорт, 1972. – 231 с.

Егоров А.С. Психологические аспекты проблемы утомления / А.С. Егоров // Теория и практика физической культуры. – 1971. – № 4. – С. 32-34.

Журавлева Н.В. Влияние специальных упражнений на точность воспроизведения различных характеристик движения / Н.В. Журавлева // Материалы конференции молодых ученых ЦНИИФК. – М., 1965. – С. 25-27.

Зациорский В.М. Исследование переноса тренированности в циклических локомоциях: автореф. дис. ... канд. пед. наук / В.М. Зациорский; ГДОИФК им. П.Ф. Лесгафта. – Л., 1961. – 15 с.

Зациорский В.М. Физические качества спортсмена / В.М. Зациорский. – М.: Физкультура и спорт, 1966. – 200 с.

Зациорский В.М. Взаимосвязь между техникой и двигательными качествами спортсменов / В.М. Зациорский. – М., ГЦОЛИФК, 1969. – 78 с.

Зациорский В.М., Казаков П.Н., Смирнов Г.А. Факторы, влияющие на точность ударов футболистов / В.М. Зациорский, П.Н. Казаков, Г.А. Смирнов // Теория и практика физической культуры. – 1975. – № 5. – С. 15-20.

Зеленцов А.М., Лобановский В.В. Моделирование тренировки в футболе / А.М. Зеленцов, В.В. Лобановский. – Киев: Здоров'я, 1985. – 134 с.

Зонин Г.С. Исследование физической, технической подготовленности и их совершенствования у футболистов: автореф. дис. ... канд. пед. наук / Г.С. Зонин; ГДОИФК им. П.Ф. Лесгафта. – Л., 1974. – 21 с.

Ивойлов А.В. Средства и методы обеспечения функциональной устойчивости точностных движений в спортивной деятельности: автореф. дис. ... докт. пед. наук / А.В. Ивойлов; МОГИФК. – Малаховка, 1987. – 51 с.

Иманалиев Т.Т. Сопряженная физическая и технико-тактическая подготовка футболистов на этапе спортивного совершенствования: автореф. дис. ... канд. пед. наук / Т.Т. Иманалиев; ЦНИИ Спорта. – М., 1993. – 24 с.

Искусство подготовки высококлассных футболистов: Научно-методическое пособие / Под ред. Н.М. Люкшинова. – М.: Советский спорт, 2003. – 416 с.

Казиев М.Х. Двигательные действия, связанные с реакцией на движущийся объект (летящий мяч), и некоторые пути повышения их эффективности: автореф. дис. ... канд. пед. наук / М.Х. Казиев; ГЦОЛИФК. – М., 1989. – 24 с.

Климин В.П. Техника. Как ее оценить? / В.П. Климин // Еженедельник «Футбол-хоккей».– 1982. – № 39. – С. 14.

Коц Я.М. Основные физиологические принципы тренировки: учеб. пособие для студентов ГЦОЛИФКа / Я.М. Коц. – М., 1986. – 36 с.

Кряж В.Н. Исследование динамики переноса тренированности в процессе тренировки: автореф. дис. ... канд. пед. наук / В.Н. Кряж; ГЦОЛИФК. – М., 1969. – 17 с.

Кураж В.П. Формирование у школьников техники игры в футбол на основе развития целевой точности движений: автореф. дис. ... канд. пед. наук / В.П. Кураж; ВНИИФК. – М., 2006. – 19 с.

Луэй Ганим Саид. Формирование специальных навыков ударных движений у футболистов различных возрастных групп: автореф. дис. ... канд. пед. наук / Луэй Ганим Саид; КГИФК. – Киев, 1983. – 24 с.

Люкшинов Н.М., Шамардин В.Н. Несоответствие игры и тренировки / Н.М. Люкшинов, В.Н. Шамардин // Еженедельник «Футбол-Хоккей». – 1978. – № 2. – С. 8.

Матвеев Л.П. Теория и методика физической культуры: учебник для ин-тов физ. культуры / Л.П. Матвеев. – М.: Физкультура и спорт, 1991. – 543 с.

Моногаров В.Д. Утомление в спорте / В.Д. Моногаров. – Киев.: Здоровье. – 1986. – 120 с.

Пагиев В.П. Исследование взаимосвязи уровня физической подготовленности и тактико-технического мастерства футболистов высших разрядов: автореф. дис. ... канд. пед. наук / В.П. Пагиев; ВНИИФК. – М., 1977. – 21 с.

Персон Р.С. Мышцы – антагонисты в движениях человека / Р.С. Персон. – М.: Наука, 1965. – 115 с.

Персон Р.С. Электромиография в исследованиях человека / Р.С. Персон. – М.: Наука, 1969. – 231 с.

Платонов В.Н. Теория и методика спортивной тренировки / В.Н. Платонов. – Киев: Вища школа, 1984. – 336 с.

Попов А.В. Совершенствование технической подготовки футболистов с учетом типов ударных движений и условий игровой деятельности: автореф. дис. ... канд. пед. наук / А.В. Попов; КГИФК. – Киев, 1981. – 24 с.

Решитько В. Точность плюс скорость / В. Решитько // Еженедельник «Футбол-Хоккей». – 1988. – № 12. – С. 12-13.

Розенблат В.В. Проблема утомления / В.В. Розенблат. – М.: Медицина, 1975. – 239 с.

Рымашевский Г.А. Экспериментальное обоснование некоторых путей повышения надежности выполнения технико-тактических действий футболистами высокой квалификации: автореф. дис. ... канд. пед. наук / Г.А. Рымашевский; ВНИИФК. – М., 1978. – 22 с.

Седов Ю.С. Исследование методов совершенствования точности пространственной и силовой дифференцировок в сложных действиях футболистов: автореф. дис. ... канд. пед. наук / Ю.С. Седов; ГДОИФК им. П.Ф. Лесгафта. – Л., 1968. – 18 с.

Селуянов В.Н., Сарсания С.К., Сарсания К.С. Физическая подготовка футболистов / В.Н. Селуянов, С.К. Сарсания. К.С. Сарсания. – М.: ТВТ Дивизион, 2006. – 192 с.

Селуянов В. и др. Футбол. Проблемы технической подготовки / В. Селуянов, Шестаков М., Диас С., Ферейра М. – М.: ТВТ Дивизион, 2009. – 104 с.

Сергиенко Л.П. Исследование влияния наследственных и средовых факторов на развитие двигательных качеств человека: автореф. дисс. ... канд. пед. наук / Л.П. Сергиенко; ГЦОЛИФК. – М., 1975. – 25 с.

Смирнов Г.А. Исследование факторов, влияющих на меткость ударов футболистов, и некоторые пути воспитания ее: автореф. дис. ... канд. пед. наук / Г.А. Смирнов; ГЦОЛИФК. – М., 1975. – 24 с.

Смирнов Г.А. О некоторых путях совершенствования точности ударов / Г.А. Смирнов // Футбол: ежегодник 1981. – М.: Физкультура и спорт, 1981. – С. 13.

Сысоев Н.В. Исследование точности движений и ее совершенствование: автореф. дис. ... канд. пед. наук / Н.В. Сысоев; ГДОИФК им. П.Ф. Лесгафта. – Л., 1963. – 18 с.

Фарфель В.С. Управление движениями в спорте / В.С. Фарфель. – М.: Физкультура и спорт, 1975. – 208 с.

Хасан Ясир Хашим. Методика повышения скорости и точности действий футболистов 18-19 лет (на опыте подготовки сборной молодежной Ирака к международным соревнованиям): автореф. дис. ... канд. пед. наук / Хасан Ясир Хашим; СПбГУФК им. П.Ф. Лесгафта. – СПб., 2005. – 24 с.

Чирва Б.Г. Футбол. Методика совершенствования «техники эпизодов игры»: учеб. пособие для студентов высших учебных заведений / Б.Г. Чирва. – М.: ТВТ Дивизион, 2006. – 112 с.

Чирва Б.Г. Основные положения переноса тренированности в быстроте и точности действий с мячом в футболе / Б.Г. Чирва // Физическая культура: воспитание, образование, тренировка. – 2008. – № 3. – С. 30-32.

Чирва Б.Г. Футбол. Концепция технической и тактической подготовки футболистов / Б.Г. Чирва. – М.: ТВТ Дивизион, 2008. – 336 с.

Чхаидзе Л.В. Об управлении движениями человека / Л.В. Чхаидзе. – М.: физкультура и спорт, 1970. – 135 с.

Шварц В.В. К проблеме врожденного и приобретенного в развитии двигательных способностей человека. – М.: Наука, 1978. – С. 155-170.

www.ingramcontent.com/pod-product-compliance
Lightning Source LLC
Chambersburg PA
CBHW060834050426
42453CB00008B/695